MODERN KNITS
Vintage Style

CLASSIC DESIGNS FROM THE GOLDEN AGE OF KNITTING

Kari Cornell, Editor

Photography by Jennifer Simonson

Voyageur Press

First published in 2010 by MBI Publishing Company LLC and Voyageur
Press, an imprint of MBI Publishing Company, 400 First Avenue North,
Suite 300, Minneapolis, MN, 55401 USA

MBI Publishing Company titles are also available at discounts in bulk
quantity for industrial or sales-promotional use. For details write to
Special Sales Manager at MBI Publishing Company, 400 First Avenue
North, Suite 300, Minneapolis, MN, 55401 USA.

ISBN-13: 978-0-7603-3679-3

ISBN-10: 0-7603-3679-2

Editor: Kari Cornell
Technical Editor: Charlotte Quiggle
Copy Editor: Betty Christiansen
Design Manager: LeAnn Kuhlmann
Designer: Sarah Bennett
Photographer: Jennifer Simonson
Stylist: London Nelson

Printed in China

Library of Congress Cataloging-in-Publication Data

Modern knits, vintage style : classic designs from the golden age of
knitting / Kari Cornell, editor ; photographs by Jennifer Simonson.

   p. cm.

  Includes index.

  ISBN 978-0-7603-3679-3 (plc)

  1. Knitting—Patterns. I. Cornell, Kari A.

  TT825.M598 2010

  746.43'2041—dc22

          2010004831

Acknowledgments I owe a big thank-you to photographer Jennifer Simonson and stylist London Nelson, who brought these fabulous knits to life, giving each shot just the right look. Many thanks to Charlotte Quiggle, our technical editor, and copyeditor Betty Christiansen, for their diligence and careful attention to detail. Thanks to Suzyn Jackson for lending the lovely 1930s child's capelette from which the design for the Charming Shoulderette was created. Kudos and thanks are in order for sample knitters Tina Melvin, who knit the Charming Shoulderette, and Rebecca Yaker, who knit the Favorite Cardigan. Lastly, I'm grateful to all of the talented designers who submitted ideas for this book.

Contents

Introduction

As a knitter who loves fashion with a vintage sensibility, I owe a great debt to actress Lana Turner. Had she not worn the legendary curve-hugging sweater in the 1939 movie *They Won't Forget*, the quintessential sweater girl of the 1940s may not have existed. As young, trendsetting women of the late 1930s and 1940s sought out fashions that mimicked Turner's sultry look, they turned to knitting. During this time, which became known as the Golden Age of Knitting, yarn companies published countless patterns for beautifully designed sweaters, skirts, hats, scarves, gloves, and more in an effort to sell their yarns.

It was paging through a stack of these old pattern leaflets and dreaming of the fantastic fashions worn by the starlets of the silver screen that inspired me to create this book. I wanted to publish a collection of patterns that captures the essence of the designs from knitting's Golden Age—the late 1930s, 1940s, and early 1950s—but features patterns by favorite contemporary designers using modern yarns that knit up at a gauge that is tempting for today's knitter. *Modern Knits, Vintage Style* does just that. Classic sweater sets, pencil skirts, and the close-fitting short-sleeve pullover all make a comeback on the pages of this book. These styles have staying power; they are the kind of pieces that can be dressed up or down and never go out of fashion.

I'm honored to be able to include the patterns of so many knitwear designers who share my love of vintage style: Anna Bell, Lily Chin, Teva Durham, Franklin Habit, Elanor Lynn, Michele Rose Orne, Annie Modesitt, Kristin Spurkland, Melissa Wehrle, and many others. It is their inspired designs that give new life to these classic garments.

I hope you enjoy knitting the patterns from this book, but most of all, I hope you like the trip down memory lane. Photos of the vintage knitwear that inspired the designs appear alongside the patterns. I loved discovering the timeless details designers chose to include and the updates they decided to incorporate. I've also included any sketches the designers provided with their projects. These sketches give a sense of the process and lend a vintage scrapbook feel to the book.

Cherry Short-Sleeve Cardigan

Design by Anna Bell

A sweet summer cardigan with slightly puffed sleeves, defined at the waist with a drawstring tie. Textured with an all-over "little birds" cable pattern, this sweater is fun to wear with a full, flippy skirt, capri pants, or a style like Katherine Hepburn with Oxford bags.

Sizes

To fit bust size 32 (34, 36, 38, 40)"/81.5 (86.5, 91.5, 96.5, 101.5)cm

Instructions are given for smallest size, with larger sizes in parentheses. When only 1 number is given, it applies to all sizes.

Finished Measurements

Circumference: 33½ (35, 37, 39½, 41½)"/85 (89, 94, 100.5, 105.5)cm

Length: 23 (23¼, 23½, 24¼, 24½)"/58.5 (50, 59.5, 61.5, 62)cm

Materials

- Jo Sharp *Soho Summer* (DK weight; 100% cotton; 109 yd/100m per 1¾ oz/50g ball): 6 (6, 7, 7, 8) balls Carmen #221
- Size 3 (3.25mm) needles
- Size 6 (4mm) needles or size needed to obtain gauge
- Five ¾" (2cm) buttons
- Tapestry needle
- 70" (178cm) ribbon in coordinating color (optional)
- 4 small snap fasteners (optional)
- Sewing thread in matching color (optional)
- Sewing needle (optional)

Gauge

22 sts and 30 rows = 4" (10cm) in cable pattern using larger needles (blocked).

Adjust needle size as necessary to obtain correct gauge.

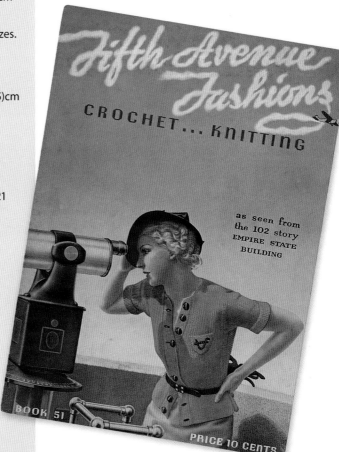

Pattern Notes

- This sweater is designed to have 1" (2.5cm) positive ease.

- Always slip sts purlwise with yarn held to WS.

- Maintain 2 selvedge sts in St st at each edge.

- If there are not enough sts to work complete 3-st cable, work in St st instead.

Special Abbreviations

1/2 RC (1 over 2 Right Cross): Slip 2 sts to cn and hold in back; k1, k2 from cn.

1/2 LC (1 over 2 Left Cross): Slip 1 st to cn and hold in front; k2, k1 from cn.

sssk: [Slip 1 st knitwise] 3 times from LH needle to RH needle, insert LH needle tip into fronts of both slipped sts, knit both sts together from this position (left-leaning double decrease).

ssp: [Slip 1 st knitwise] twice from LH needle to RH needle, return both sts to LH needle and purl both together through back loops (left-leaning decrease).

M1L (Make 1 Left): Insert LH needle from front to back under the running thread between the last st worked and next st on LH needle; knit into the back of resulting loop.

M1R (Make 1 Right): Insert LH needle from back to front under the running thread between the last st worked and next st on LH needle. With RH needle, knit into the front of resulting loop.

Special Technique

1-Row, 3-St Buttonhole: With RS facing, work to desired position for buttonhole. Bring yarn to front and sl 1 pwise, then bring yarn to back of work; *sl 1 pwise, pass the 2nd slipped st over the first as if to BO; rep from * twice (3 sts bound off); slip last st on RH needle back to LH needle. Turn work. Using cable method, CO 4 sts on LH needle; turn work. Slip first st on LH needle pwise, then pass the last cast-on st over this st. Continue knitting.

Stitch Pattern

Little Birds Cable Pattern (multiple of 14 sts)

Row 1 (RS): *K6, sl 2, k6; rep from * across.

Row 2: *P6, sl 2, p6; rep from * across.

Row 3: *K4, 1/2 RC, 1/2 LC, K4; rep from * across.

Row 4: Purl.

Row 5: Knit.

Row 6: Purl.

Row 7: *Sl 1, k12, sl 1; rep from * across.

Row 8: *Sl 1, p12, sl 1; rep from * across.

Row 9: *1/2 LC, k8, 1/2 RC; rep from * across.

Rows 10–12: Rep Rows 4–6.

Rep Rows 1–12 for pat.

Instructions

BACK

With smaller needles, CO 91 (97, 103, 109, 115) sts.

Row 1 (RS): K1, *k1, p1; rep from * to last 2 sts, k2.

Row 2: P2, *K1, p1; rep from * to last st, p1.

Cont in est rib until piece measures 1½" (4cm), ending with a WS row, and on last row, inc 1 st in middle of row—94 (98, 104, 110, 116) sts.

Change to larger needles.

Pat set-up row (RS): K5 (0, 3, 6, 2), beg pat where indicated on Chart for size being worked, work in Little Birds Cable pat to last 5 (0, 3, 6, 2) sts, knit to end.

Work 5 rows even in est pat.

Waist shaping

Dec row (RS): K2, k2tog, work to last 4 sts, ssk, k2—92 (96, 102, 108, 114) sts.

Maintaining pat but eliminating pat at edge where necessary, rep Dec row [every 6 rows] 3 times, then [every 4 rows] twice—82 (86, 92, 98, 104) sts.

Work 3 rows even, ending with Row 10 of pat.

Waist detail

Change to smaller needles and purl 2 rows.

Eyelet row (RS): K1 (0, 1, 1, 2), *k2, yo, k2tog, k1; rep from * to last 1 (1, 2, 2) sts, k1 (1, 1, 2, 2).

Purl 3 rows.

Bust shaping

Change to larger needles and beg with Row 5 of pat, work even for 6 rows.

Inc row (RS): K2, M1R, work in pat to last 2 sts, M1L, k2—84 (88, 94, 100, 106) sts.

Rep Inc row [every 6 rows] once, then [every 8 rows] 3 times—92 (96, 102, 108, 114) sts.

Work even until piece measures 15 (15, 15, 15½, 15½)", ending with a WS row.

Shape armholes

Next 2 rows: Maintaining pat, BO 3 (3, 4, 4, 5) sts, work to end—86 (90, 94, 100, 104) sts.

Dec row (RS): K2, k2tog, work in pat to last 4 sts, ssk, k2—84 (88, 92, 98, 102) sts.

Dec row (WS): P2, ssp, work in pat to last 4 sts, p2tog, p2—82 (86, 90, 96, 100) sts.

Cont to dec each side [every row] 1 (1, 1, 3, 4) more time(s), then [every other row] 3 (4, 5, 5, 5) times, then [every 4 rows] once—72 (74, 76, 78, 80) sts.

Work even until armhole measures 7 (7¼, 7½, 7¾, 8)"/18 (18.5, 19, 19.5, 20.5)cm, ending with a WS row.

Shape back neck and shoulders

Row 1 (RS): Work 24 (24, 25, 25, 26) sts, join a 2nd ball of yarn and BO center 24 (26, 26, 28, 28) sts, work 24 (24, 25, 25, 26) sts.

Rows 2–5: BO 4 sts at each neck edge twice and work rem sts in pat—16 (16, 17, 17, 18) sts rem each side.

Rows 6 and 7: Dec 1 st at each neck edge as for armhole—14 (14, 15, 15, 16) sts rem each side.

BO 7 (7, 8, 8, 8) sts at beg of next 2 rows, then 7 (7, 7, 7, 8) sts at beg of following 2 rows.

LEFT FRONT

With smaller needles, CO 45 (47, 49, 53, 55) sts.

Row 1 (RS): K1, *k1, p1; rep from * to last 2 sts, k2.

Row 2: P2, *k1, p1; rep from * to last st, p1.

Cont in est rib until piece measures 1½" (4cm), ending with a WS row.

Change to larger needles.

Pat set-up row (RS): K5 (0, 3, 6, 2), beg pat where indicated on Chart for size being worked, work in Little Birds Cable pat to last 4 sts, k4.

Work 5 rows even in est pat.

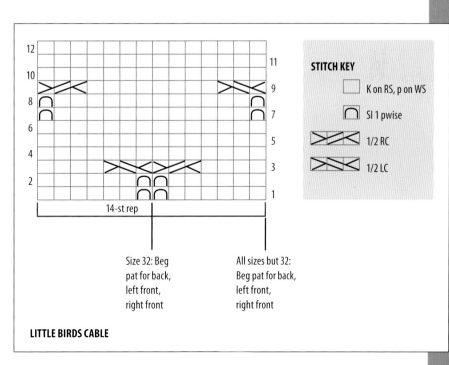

STITCH KEY

	K on RS, p on WS
	Sl 1 pwise
	1/2 RC
	1/2 LC

14-st rep

Size 32: Beg pat for back, left front, right front

All sizes but 32: Beg pat for back, left front, right front

LITTLE BIRDS CABLE

Waist shaping

Dec row (RS): K2, k2tog, work in pat to end—44 (46, 48, 52, 54) sts.

Maintaining pat but eliminating pat at edge where necessary, rep Dec row [every 6 rows] 3 times, then [every 4 rows] twice—39 (41, 43, 47, 49) sts.

Work 3 rows even, ending with Row 10 of pat.

Waist detail

Change to smaller needles and purl 2 rows.

Eyelet row (RS): K2 (2, 2, 3, 3), *k2tog, yo, k3; rep from * to last 2 (4, 1, 4, 1) sts, [k2] ([k2tog, yo, k2], [k1], [k2tog, yo, k2], [k1]).

Purl 3 rows.

Bust shaping

Change to larger needles and beg with Row 5 of pat, work even for 6 rows.

Inc row (RS): K2, M1R, work in pat to to end—40 (42, 44, 48, 50) sts.

Rep Inc row [every 6 rows] once, then [every 8 rows] 3 times—44 (46, 48, 52, 54) sts.

Work even until piece measures 15 (15, 15, 15½, 15½)", ending with a WS row.

Shape armhole

Next row (RS): Maintaining pat, BO 3 (3, 4, 4, 5) sts, work to end—41 (43, 44, 48, 49) sts.

Work 1 row even.

Dec row (RS): K2, k2tog, work in pat to end—40 (42, 43, 47, 48) sts.

Dec row (WS): Work in pat to last 4 sts, p2tog, p2—39 (41, 42, 46, 47) sts.

Cont to dec at armhole edge [every row] 1 (1, 1, 3, 4) more time(s), then [every other row] 3 (4, 5, 5, 5) times, then [every 4 rows] once—34 (35, 35, 37, 37) sts.

Work even until armhole measures 3 (3, 3½, 3½, 4)"/7.5 (7.5, 9, 10)cm, ending with a RS row.

Shape neck and shoulder

Next row (WS): BO 5 sts, work in pat to end—29 (30, 30, 32, 32) sts.

BO 3 sts at beg of next 2 WS rows—23 (24, 24, 26, 26) sts.

Dec row (RS): Work to last 4 sts, ssk, k2—22 (23, 23, 25, 25) sts.

Dec row (WS): P2, ssp, work to end—21 (22, 22, 24, 24) sts.

Rep RS Dec row on next row, then [every other row] 6 (7, 6, 8, 7) times—14 (14, 15, 15, 16) sts rem.

Work even until armhole measures 8 (8¼, 8½, 8¾, 9)", ending with a WS row.

Next row (RS): BO 7 (7, 8, 8, 8) sts, work to end—7 (7, 7, 7, 8) sts.

Work 1 row even.

BO rem sts.

RIGHT FRONT

With smaller needles, CO 45 (47, 49, 53, 55) sts.

Row 1 (RS): K1, *k1, p1; rep from * to last 2 sts, k2.

Row 2: P2, *k1, p1; rep from * to last st, p1.

Cont in est rib until piece measures 1½" (4cm), ending with a WS row.

Change to larger needles.

Pat set-up row (RS): K5 (5, 4, 5, 3), beg pat where indicated on Chart for size being worked, work in Little Birds Cable pat to last 4 sts, k4.

Work 5 rows even in est pat.

Waist shaping

Dec row (RS): Work in pat to last 4 sts, ssk, k2—44 (46, 48, 52, 54) sts.

Maintaining pat but eliminating pat at edge where necessary, rep Dec row [every 6 rows] 3 times, then [every 4 rows] twice—39 (41, 43, 47, 49) sts.

Work 3 rows even, ending with Row 10 of pat.

Waist detail

Change to smaller needles and purl 2 rows.

Eyelet row (RS): K5 (2, 4, 2, 4) *yo, k2tog, k3; rep from * to last 4 (4, 4, 0, 0) sts, [yo, k2tog, k2] ([yo, k2tog, k2], [yo, k2tog, k2], —, —).

Purl 3 rows.

Bust shaping

Change to larger needles and beg with Row 5 of pat, work even for 6 rows.

Inc row (RS): Work to last 2 sts, M1L, k2—40 (42, 44, 48, 50) sts.

Rep Inc row [every 6 rows] once, then [every 8 rows] 3 times—44 (46, 48, 52, 54) sts.

Work even until piece measures 15 (15, 15, 15½, 15½)", ending with a RS row.

Shape armhole

Next row (WS): Maintaining pat, BO 3 (3, 4, 4, 5) sts, work to end—41 (43, 44, 48, 49) sts.

Dec row (RS): Work in pat to last 4 sts, ssk, k2—40 (42, 43, 47, 48) sts.

Dec row (WS): P2, ssp, work in pat to end—39 (41, 42, 46, 47) sts.

Cont to dec at armhole edge [every row] 1 (1, 1, 3, 4) more time(s), then [every other row] 3 (4, 5, 5, 5) times, then [every 4 rows] once—34 (35, 35, 37, 37) sts.

Work even until armhole measures 3 (3, 3½, 3½, 4)"/7.5 (7.5, 9, 10)cm, ending with a WS row.

Shape neck and shoulder

Next row (RS): BO 5 sts, work in pat to end—29 (30, 30, 32, 32) sts.

BO 3 sts at beg of next 2 RS rows—23 (24, 24, 26, 26) sts.

Dec row (RS): K2, k2tog, work in pat to end—22 (23, 23, 25, 25) sts.

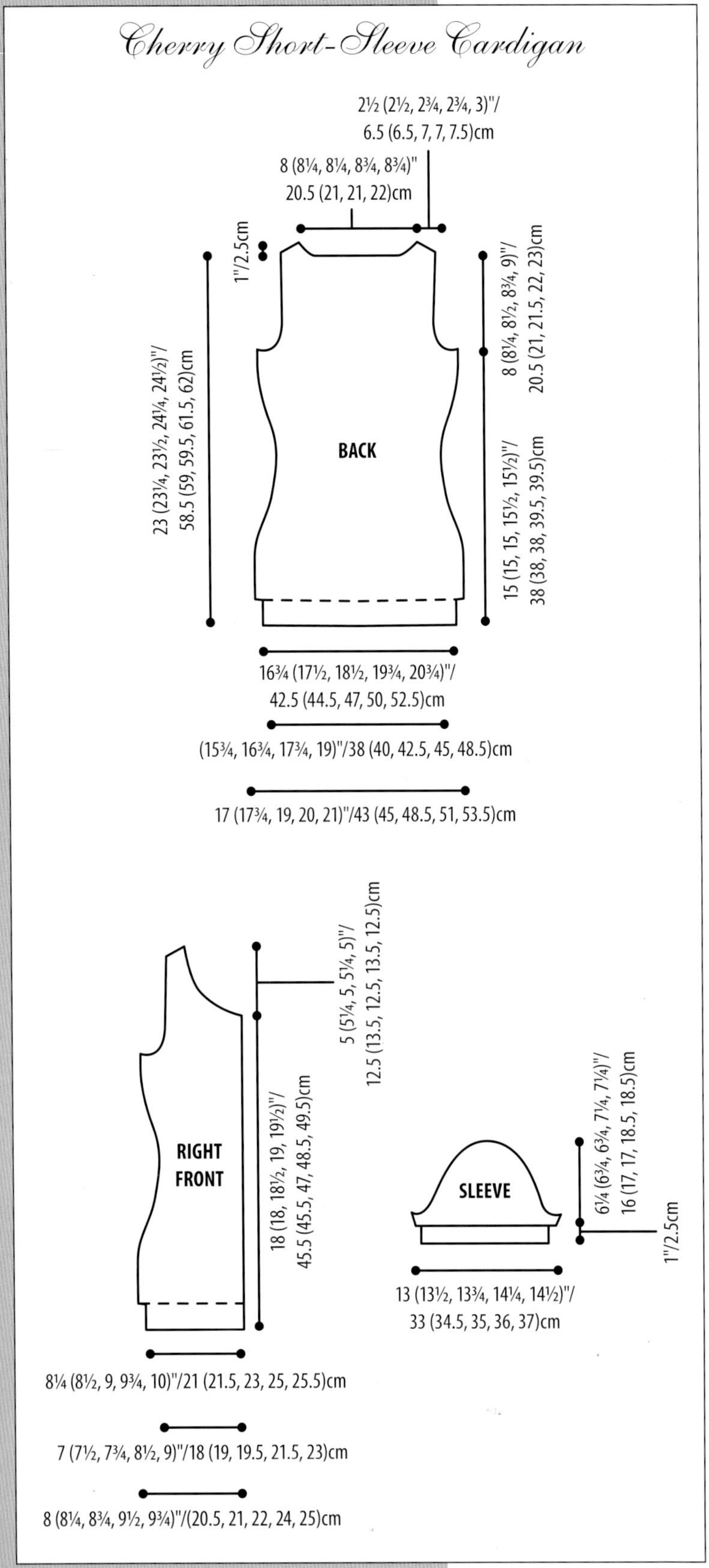
Cherry Short-Sleeve Cardigan
2½ (2½, 2¾, 2¾, 3)"/
6.5 (6.5, 7, 7, 7.5)cm
8 (8¼, 8¼, 8¾, 8¾)"
20.5 (21, 21, 22)cm
1"/2.5cm
23 (23¼, 23½, 24¼, 24½)"/
58.5 (59, 59.5, 61.5, 62)cm
BACK
8 (8¼, 8½, 8¾, 9)"/
20.5 (21, 21.5, 22, 23)cm
15 (15, 15, 15½, 15½)"/
38 (38, 38, 39.5, 39.5)cm
16¾ (17½, 18½, 19¾, 20¾)"/
42.5 (44.5, 47, 50, 52.5)cm
(15¾, 16¾, 17¾, 19)"/38 (40, 42.5, 45, 48.5)cm
17 (17¾, 19, 20, 21)"/43 (45, 48.5, 51, 53.5)cm
RIGHT FRONT
5 (5¼, 5, 5¼, 5)"/
12.5 (13.5, 12.5, 13.5, 12.5)cm
18 (18, 18½, 19, 19½)"/
45.5 (45.5, 47, 48.5, 49.5)cm
8¼ (8½, 9, 9¾, 10)"/21 (21.5, 23, 25, 25.5)cm
7 (7½, 7¾, 8½, 9)"/18 (19, 19.5, 21.5, 23)cm
8 (8¼, 8¾, 9½, 9¾)"/(20.5, 21, 22, 24, 25)cm
SLEEVE
6¼ (6¾, 6¾, 7¼, 7¼)"/
16 (17, 17, 18.5, 18.5)cm
1"/2.5cm
13 (13½, 13¾, 14¼, 14½)"/
33 (34.5, 35, 36, 37)cm

Dec row (WS): Work in pat to last 4 sts, p2tog, p2—21 (22, 22, 24, 24) sts.

Rep RS Dec row on next row, then [every other row] 6 (7, 6, 8, 7) times—14 (14, 15, 15, 16) sts rem.

Work even until armhole measures 8 (8¼, 8½, 8¾, 9)", ending with a RS row.

Next row (WS): BO 7 (7, 8, 8, 8) sts, work to end—7 (7, 7, 7, 8) sts.

Work 1 row even.

BO rem sts.

SLEEVES

Using smaller needles, CO 53 (55, 57, 59, 61) sts.

Row 1 (RS): K2, *p1, k1; rep from * to last st, k1.

Row 2: P2, *k1, p1; rep from * to last st, p1.

Work even in established rib until piece measures 1"/2.5cm, ending with a RS row.

Inc row (WS): P8 (9, 10, 11, 12), [p1f&b, p1] 19 times, p7 (8, 9, 10, 11)—72 (74, 76, 78, 80) sts.

Shape sleeve cap

Change to larger needles.

Beg with Row 1 of st pat, BO 3 (3, 4, 4, 5) sts at beg of next 2 rows—66 (68, 68, 70, 70) sts.

Pat set-up row/Dec row (RS): K2, k2tog, k1 (2, 2, 3, 3), *sl 1 wyib, k12, sl 1 wyib; rep from * to last 5 (6, 6, 7, 7) sts, k1 (2, 2, 3, 3), ssk, k2—64 (66, 66, 68, 68) sts.

Dec row (WS): P2, ssp, work in est pat to last 4 sts, p2tog, p2—62 (64, 64, 66, 66) sts.

Maintaining 2-st selvedges in St st, cont to dec 1 st at each edge [every RS row] 7 times, then [every other RS row] 4 (5, 5, 6, 6) times, then [every RS row] 5 times—30 sts.

Work 1 WS Dec row—28 sts.

Next row (RS): BO 4 sts, k4, [sssk, k1] 3 times, knit to end—18 sts.

Next row: BO 4 sts, work to end—14 sts.

BO rem sts.

Finishing

Weave in all ends. Block all pieces to finished measurements.

Sew shoulder seams.

Buttonband

With RS facing and smaller needles, pick up and knit 3 sts in every 4 rows evenly along left front edge.

Work in K1, P1 Rib for 7 rows.

BO loosely in rib.

Buttonhole band

Place markers along right front for 4 buttonholes, taking into account that 5th buttonhole will be on the neckband (see pictures for placement—lowest button sits just beneath eyelets at waist).

Work as for left front buttonband until 3 rows of rib have been completed.

Buttonhole row (RS): *Work in rib to marker, work a 1-Row, 3-St Buttonhole (or use your preferred method); rep from *, then work rib to end.

Work 3 more rows in rib.

BO loosely in rib.

Neckband

With RS facing and smaller needles, pick up and knit 45 (45, 47, 47, 49) sts along right front neck (including buttonhole band), 55 (55, 55, 57, 57) along back neck, and 45 (45, 47, 47, 49) sts along left front neck (including buttonband)—145 (145, 149, 151, 155) sts.

Work 2 rows in K1, P1 Rib.

Buttonhole row (WS): Work in rib to last 7 sts, work buttonhole as before, work in rib to end.

Work 3 more rows in rib.

BO loosely in rib.

Set in sleeves. Sew side and sleeve seams. Sew on buttons opposite buttonholes. If desired, sew snaps on bands between buttons.

Twisted Cord

Cut a strand of yarn approx 12 yd (11m) long. Fold in half and secure folded end to a stationary object (a doorknob is good). Twist yarn until it begins to double back on itself. Fold in half again with both ends together and allow to twist up on itself. Cut to approx 70" (178cm) or desired length and knot the ends to secure. Thread in and out of eyelets at waist.

If preferred, thread a ribbon in a coordinating color through the eyelets instead of the twisted cord.

Branching Out Scarf

Design by Susan Pierce Lawrence

The scarf was an essential part of the vintage wardrobe. This small project incorporates all of the most common increases and decreases used in lace knitting. The end result is a lovely accessory that is warm but ethereal.

Finished Measurements

Approx 6¾ x 67" (17 x 170cm) after blocking

Materials

• Shibuiknits *Silk Cloud* (lace weight; 60% kid mohair/40% silk; 330 yd/300m per 25g ball): 1 ball Mulberry #SC229

• Size 6 (4mm) needles or size needed to obtain gauge

Gauge

16 sts and 29 rows = 4" (10cm) in St st (blocked).

Adjust needle size as necessary to obtain correct gauge.

Pattern Notes

- The length of the scarf is customizable. Each repeat of the 10-row lace pattern adds approximately 1½" (4cm) to the length of the scarf.

- The lace pattern increases stitch count on Row 1 (+6 sts), then decreases stitch count on Rows 7 (-4 sts) and 9 (-2 sts).

Special Abbreviation

S2KP2 (Centered Double Decrease): Sl 2 tog knitwise, k1, p2sso.

STITCH KEY

☐	Knit
◯	YO
■	No stitch
╲	Ssk
╱	K2tog
⋀	K3tog
⋋	Sssk
⋀	S2KP2

Notes:
Chart shows RS rows only. Purl all WS rows.
Row 1 incs to 25 sts.
Row 7 decs to 21 sts.
Row 9 decs to 19 sts.

Stitch Pattern

LACE PATTERN

Row 1 (RS): Ssk, yo, k5, [yo, k1] 5 times, yo, k5, yo, k2tog—25 sts.

Row 2 and all WS rows: Purl.

Row 3: Ssk, yo, ssk, k1, [k2tog, yo] 2 times, k3, yo, k1, yo, k3, [yo, ssk] 2 times, k1, k2tog, yo, k2tog.

Row 5: Ssk, yo, k3tog, yo, k2tog, yo, k5, yo, k1, yo, k5, yo, ssk, yo, sssk, yo, k2tog.

Row 7: K3tog, yo, k2tog, yo, k1, yo, ssk, k1, k2tog, yo, S2KP2, yo, ssk, k1, k2tog, yo, k1, yo, ssk, yo, sssk—21 sts.

Row 9: K1, k2tog, yo, k3, yo, k3tog, yo, S2KP2, yo, sssk, yo, k3, yo, ssk, k1—19 sts.

Row 10: Purl.

Rep Rows 1–10 for pat.

Instructions

BORDER
Using the knit-on method, CO 27 sts.

Work 7 rows in garter st.

LACE BODY
Set-up row (RS): K4 (edge sts), pm, work Row 1 of Lace pat to last 4 sts, pm, k4—33 sts.

Working first and last 4 sts in garter st, work 40 reps of Lace pat or until scarf measures desired length.

BORDER
Work 7 rows in garter st.

Work Dec BO across all sts very loosely as follows: K1, *k1, insert the tip of the LH needle into the front of the 2 sts on the RH needle and knit them tog; rep from * until all sts are bound off.

BLOCKING AND FINISHING
Weave in all yarn ends, but do not trim them.

Soak the scarf in cool water until thoroughly wet. Gently squeeze out the excess water, then place the scarf between two towels and press firmly to remove additional water. Block to finished measurements by pinning the damp scarf on a flat surface. Do not remove the pins until the scarf is completely dry. Trim yarn ends.

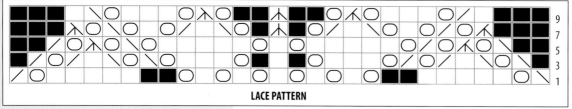

LACE PATTERN

Favorite Cardigan

Design by Anna Bell

This is a classic round-neck cardigan. The subtle and flattering vertical stripe is formed with lines of mock cable, which extend through the cuffs. Pearl buttons are the final accent.

Sizes

To fit bust size 32 (35, 38, 41, 44)"/81 (89, 96.5, 104, 112)cm

Instructions are given for smallest size, with larger sizes in parentheses. When only 1 number is given, it applies to all sizes.

Finished Measurements

Chest: 35½ (38½, 41, 44½, 47½)"/90 (98, 104, 113, 120.5)cm

Length to shoulders: 19½ (20½, 21, 22, 22½)"/49.5 (52, 53.5, 56, 57)cm

Materials

• Debbie Bliss *Cashmerino Baby* (sport weight; 55% merino wool/33% microfiber/12% cashmere; 136 yd/125m per 1¾ oz/50g ball): 10 (10, 11, 11, 12) balls Midnight Blue #008

• Size 2 (2.75mm) needles

• Size 3 (3.25mm) needles or size needed to obtain gauge

• 9 small, approx ⅜" (1cm), pearl shank buttons

• Tapestry needle

Gauge

28 sts and 36 rows = 4" (10cm) in Mock Cable pat using larger needles.

Adjust needle size as necessary to obtain correct gauge.

Abbreviations

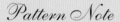

T2 (Twist 2): Knit into 2nd st on LH needle, then into first st; slip both sts off LH needle together.

M1L (Make 1 Left): Insert LH needle from front to back under the running thread between the last st worked and next st on LH needle; knit into the back of resulting loop.

M1R (Make 1 Right): Insert LH needle from back to front under the running thread between the last st worked and next st on LH needle. With RH needle, knit into the front of resulting loop.

Pattern Note

The full-fashioned decreases are worked *against* the slope of the shaping.

Stitch Pattern

MOCK CABLE RIB (multiple of 7 sts + 2)
Row 1 (WS): P2, *[k1, p1] twice, k1, p2; rep from * across.

Row 2 (RS): T2, *p1, [k1-tbl, p1] twice, T2; rep from * across.

Rep Rows 1 and 2 for pat.

MOCK CABLE (multiple of 7 sts + 2)
Row 1 (RS): T2, *k5, T2; rep from * to end.

Row 2: Purl.

Rep Rows 1 and 2 for pat.

Instructions

BACK
With smaller needles, CO 108 (118, 126, 140, 150) sts.

Pat set-up row (WS): [P1, k1] 2 (1, 3, 3, 2) times, work Mock Cable Rib to last 4 (2, 6, 6, 4) sts, [k1, p1] 2 (1, 3, 3, 2) times.

Row 2 (RS): [K1-tbl, p1] 2 (1, 3, 3, 2) times, work est Mock Cable Rib to last 4 (2, 6, 6, 4) sts, [p1, k1-tbl] 2 (1, 3, 3, 2) times.

Work even in est pat until piece measures 2" (5cm), ending with a WS row.

Next row (RS): Change to larger needles; work 4 (2, 6, 6, 4) sts in est rib, work Mock Cable pat to last 4 (2, 6, 6, 4) sts, work in est rib to end.

Work 7 rows even in est pat.

Inc row (RS): K1-tbl, M1R, work in est pat to last st, M1L, k1-tbl—110 (120, 128, 142, 152) sts.

Working new sts into rib pat, rep Inc row [every 8 (8, 8, 10, 10) rows] 7 (7, 8, 7, 7) times—124 (134, 144, 156, 166) sts.

Work even until piece measures 12 (12½, 12½, 13, 13)", ending with a WS row.

Shape armholes
BO 5 (6, 6, 7, 7) sts at beg of next 2 rows—114 (122, 132, 142, 152) sts.

Dec row (RS): K1, k2tog, work in est pat to last 3 sts, ssk, k1—112 (120, 130, 140, 150) sts.

Dec row (WS): P1, ssp, work in est pat to last 3 sts, p2tog, p1—110 (118, 128, 138, 148) sts.

Rep last 2 rows 1 (2, 2, 3, 3) times—106 (110, 120, 126, 136) sts.

Work Dec row [every RS row] 4 (4, 6, 7, 9) times—98 (102, 108, 112, 118) sts.

Work Dec row [every other RS row] 2 (2, 3, 3, 4) times—94 (98, 102, 106, 110) sts.

Work even until armholes measure 7½ (8, 8½, 9, 9 1.2)", ending with a WS row.

Shape shoulders and back neck

Mark center 30 (32, 34, 36, 38) sts for back neck.

Next row (RS): K32 (33, 34, 35, 36), join 2nd ball of yarn and BO center 30 (32, 34, 36, 38) sts, work to end of row.

Next 2 rows: Working both sides at once with separate balls of yarn, BO 9 sts at shoulder edge, work to neck edge; BO 6 sts at neck edge, work to end of row— 17 (18, 19, 20, 21) sts rem each side.

Next 2 rows: BO 9 sts at shoulder edge, work to neck edge; BO 4 sts at neck edge, work to end of row—4 (5, 6, 7, 8) sts rem.

BO rem sts.

LEFT FRONT

With smaller needles, CO 54 (59, 63, 70, 75) sts.

Set-up row (WS): [P1, k1] 2 (1, 3, 3, 2) times, work Mock Cable Rib to last 6 sts, [k1, p1] 3 times.

Row 2 (RS): [K1-tbl, p1] 3 times, work est Mock Cable Rib to last 4 (2, 6, 6, 4) sts, [p1, k1-tbl] 2 (1, 3, 3, 2) times.

Work even in est pat until piece measures 2" (5cm), ending with a WS row.

Next row (RS): Change to larger needles; work 6 sts in est rib, work Mock Cable pat to last 4 (2, 6, 6, 4) sts, work in est rib to end.

Work 7 rows even in est pat.

Inc row (RS): K1-tbl, M1R, work in est pat to end—55 (60, 64, 71, 76) sts.

Working new sts into rib pat, rep Inc row [every 8 (8, 8, 10, 10) rows] 7 (7, 8, 7, 7) times—62 (67, 72, 78, 83) sts.

Work even until piece measures same as back to underarm, ending with a WS row.

Shape armholes

Next row (RS): BO 5 (6, 6, 7, 7) sts, work in est pat to end—57 (61, 66, 71, 76) sts.

Work 1 row even.

Dec row (RS): K1, k2tog, work in est pat to end—56 (60, 65, 70, 75) sts.

Dec row (WS): Work in est pat to last 3 sts, p2tog, p1—55 (59, 64, 69, 74) sts.

Rep last 2 rows 1 (2, 2, 3, 3) times—53 (55, 60, 63, 68) sts.

Work Dec row [every RS row] 4 (4, 6, 7, 9) times—49 (51, 54, 56, 59) sts.

Work Dec row [every other RS row] 2 (2, 3, 3, 4) times—47 (49, 51, 53, 55) sts.

Work even until armhole measures 4 (4½, 5, 5½, 6)"/10 (11.5, 12.5, 14, 15)cm, ending with a RS row.

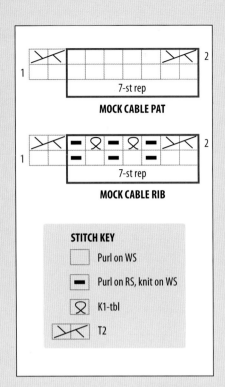

MOCK CABLE PAT

MOCK CABLE RIB

7-st rep

Shape front neck and shoulders

Next row (WS): BO 10 (10, 11, 11, 12) sts, work in est pat to end—37 (39, 40, 42, 43) sts.

Dec row (RS): Work to last 3 sts, ssk, k1—36 (38, 39, 41, 42) sts.

Dec row (WS): P1, ssp, work in est pat to end—35 (37, 38, 40, 41) sts.

Rep last 2 rows 3 times, then dec [every RS row] 7 (8, 8, 9, 9) times—22 (23, 24, 25, 26) sts. Work even until armhole measures 7½ (8, 8½, 9, 9½)", ending with a WS row.

BO 9 sts at beg of next 2 RS rows, then BO rem 4 (5, 6, 7, 8) sts on following RS row.

RIGHT FRONT

With smaller needles, CO 54 (59, 63, 70, 75) sts.

Set-up row (WS): [P1, k1] 3 times, work Mock Cable Rib to last 4 (2, 6, 6, 4) sts, [p1, k1] 2 (1, 3, 3, 2) times.

Row 2 (RS): [K1-tbl, p1] 2 (1, 3, 3, 2) times, work est Mock Cable Rib to last 6 sts, [p1, k1-tbl] 3 times.

Work even in est pat until piece measures 2" (5cm), ending with a WS row.

Next row (RS): Change to larger needles; work 4 (2, 6, 6, 4) sts in est rib, work Mock Cable pat to last 6 sts, work in est rib to end.

Work 7 rows even in est pat.

Inc row (RS): Work to last st, M1L, k1-tbl—55 (60, 64, 71, 76) sts.

Working new sts into rib pat, rep Inc row [every 8 (8, 8, 10, 10) rows] 7 (7, 8, 7, 7) times—62 (67, 72, 78, 83) sts.

Work even until piece measures same as back to underarm, ending with a RS row.

Shape armholes

Next row (WS): BO 5 (6, 6, 7, 7) sts, work in est pat to end—57 (61, 66, 71, 76) sts.

Dec row (RS): Work in est pat to last 3 sts, ssk, k1—56 (60, 65, 70, 75) sts.

Dec row (WS): P1, ssp, work in est pat to end—55 (59, 64, 69, 74) sts.

Rep last 2 rows 1 (2, 2, 3, 3) times—53 (55, 60, 63, 68) sts.

Work Dec row [every RS row] 4 (4, 6, 7, 9) times—49 (51, 54, 56, 59) sts.

Work Dec row [every other RS row] 2 (2, 3, 3, 4) times—47 (49, 51, 53, 55) sts.

Work even until armhole measures 4 (4½, 5, 5½, 6)")/10 (11.5, 12.5, 14, 15)cm, ending with a WS row.

Shape front neck and shoulders

Next row (RS): BO 10 (10, 11, 11, 12) sts, work in pat to end—37 (39, 40, 42, 43) sts.

Dec row (WS): Work in pat to last 3 sts, p2tog, p1—36 (38, 39, 41, 42) sts.

Dec row (RS): K1, k2tog, work in pat to end—35 (37, 38, 40, 41) sts.

Rep last 2 rows 3 times, then dec [every WS row] 7 (8, 8, 9, 9) times—22 (23, 24, 25, 26) sts.

Favorite Cardigan

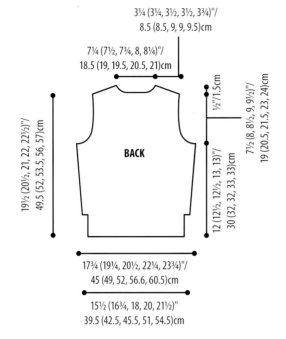

3¼ (3¼, 3½, 3½, 3¾)"/
8.5 (8.5, 9, 9, 9.5)cm

7¼ (7½, 7¾, 8, 8¼)"/
18.5 (19, 19.5, 20.5, 21)cm

½"/1.5cm

7½ (8, 8½, 9, 9½)"/
19 (20.5, 21.5, 23, 24)cm

BACK

19½ (20½, 21, 22, 22½)"/
49.5 (52, 53.5, 56, 57)cm

12 (12½, 12½, 13, 13)"/
30 (32, 32, 33, 33)cm

17¾ (19¼, 20½, 22¼, 23¾)"/
45 (49, 52, 56.6, 60.5)cm

15½ (16¾, 18, 20, 21½)"
39.5 (42.5, 45.5, 51, 54.5)cm

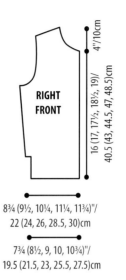

4"/10cm

**RIGHT
FRONT**

16 (17, 17½, 18½, 19)/
40.5 (43, 44.5, 47, 48.5)cm

8¾ (9½, 10¼, 11¼, 11¾)"/
22 (24, 26, 28.5, 30)cm

7¾ (8½, 9, 10, 10¾)"/
19.5 (21.5, 23, 25.5, 27.5)cm

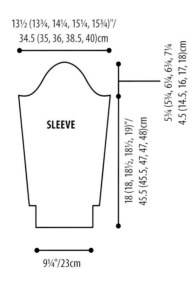

13½ (13¾, 14¼, 15¼, 15¾)"/
34.5 (35, 36, 38.5, 40)cm

5¾ (5¾, 6¼, 6¾, 7¼)"/
14.5, 16, 17, 18)cm

SLEEVE

18 (18, 18½, 18½, 19)"/
45.5 (45.5, 47, 47, 48)cm

9¼"/23cm

Work even until armhole measures 7½ (8, 8½, 9, 9½)", ending with a RS row.

BO 9 sts at beg of next 2 WS rows, then BO rem 4 (5, 6, 7, 8) sts on following WS row.

SLEEVES
With smaller needles, CO 64 sts.

Row 1 (WS): P2, k1; work Mock Cable Rib to last 3 sts, k1, p2.

Row 2 (RS): K2, p1; work Mock Cable Rib to last 3 sts, p1, k2.

Work even in est pat until piece measures 2" (5cm), ending with a WS row.

Next row (RS): Change to larger needles; k3, work Mock Cable pat to last 3 sts, k3.

Work even in est pat for 5 rows.

Inc row (RS): K1, M1R, work in est pat to last st, M1L, k1—66 sts.

Maintaining first and last sts in St st and working new sts into pat as they accumulate, rep Inc row [every 8 (8, 6, 6, 6) rows] 14 (15, 17, 20, 22) times—94 (96, 100, 106, 110) sts.

Work even until piece measures 18 (18, 18½, 18½, 19)", ending with a WS row.

Shape sleeve caps
Maintaining pat, BO 5 (6, 6, 7, 7) sts at beg of next 2 rows—84 (84, 88, 92, 96) sts.

Dec row (RS): K1, k2tog, work in est pat to last 3 sts, ssk, k1—82 (82, 86, 90, 94) sts.

Dec row (WS): P1, ssp, work in est pat to last 3 sts, p2tog, p1—80 (80, 84, 88, 92) sts.

Rep last 2 rows 2 (1, 1, 3, 3) time(s)—74 (76, 80, 76, 80) sts.

Work Dec row [every RS row] 6 (7, 8, 5, 6) times—62 (62, 64, 66, 68) sts.

Work Dec row [every other RS row] 4 (4, 4, 6, 6) times—54 (54, 56, 54, 56) sts.

Work Dec row [every RS row] 6 (6, 7, 6, 7) times—42 sts.

Work 1 WS row even.

Work Dec row [every row] twice—38 sts.

BO 5 sts at beg of next 2 rows—28 sts.

BO rem sts.

Finishing

Weave in all ends. Block all pieces to finished measurements.

Buttonband
With RS facing and using smaller needles, pick up and knit 116 (123, 127, 134, 138) sts evenly along left front edge.

Work 8 rows in K1, P1 Rib.

BO in rib.

Buttonhole band

Place markers for 8 buttonholes along right front, bearing in mind that the top (9th) buttonhole will be on the neckband (see pictures for placement).

Pick up and knit as for buttonband.

Work 3 rows in K1, P1 Rib.

Buttonhole row (RS): Maintaining est rib, work buttonholes (k2tog, yo) opposite markers.

Work 4 more rows in rib.

BO in rib.

Sew shoulder seams.

Neckband

With RS facing and using smaller needles, pick up and knit 44 (46, 46, 48, 48) sts along right front neck (including buttonhole band), 54 (56, 58, 60, 62) sts around back neck, and 44 (46, 46, 48, 48) sts along left front neck (including buttonband)—142 (148, 150, 156, 158) sts.

Work 1 row of K1, P1 Rib.

Next row (RS): Work 4 sts rib, make buttonhole (k2tog, yo), rib to end.

Work 3 more rows in rib.

BO in rib.

Set in sleeves. Sew side and sleeve seams.

Sew on buttons opposite buttonholes.

Waves Pullover

Design by Elanor Lynn

I designed this tight-fitting pullover to go with jeans or, more classically, with a simple pencil skirt, such as the Pennant Pleated Skirt (page 38). The vintage jewel neckline requires a three-button closure in the back to be able to fit around the head. Please note that the sizing is small because it is intended to fit quite tightly, at least two to three inches smaller than you actually measure—even up to five or six inches smaller!

Sizes

Fits up to a 35 (38, 41)"/89 (96.5, 104)cm bust.

Instructions are given for smallest size, with larger sizes in parentheses. When only 1 number is given, it applies to all sizes.

Finished Measurements

Bust: 30 (33, 36)"/76 (84, 91.5)cm

Length: 19 (20¼, 22)"/48.5 (51.5, 56)cm

Materials 4

- Cascade *220* (worsted weight; 100% wool; 220 yd/100g per skein): 5 (6, 7) skeins red #9404
- Size 2 (2.75mm) 24" (60cm) circular needle
- Size 5 (3.75mm) 24" (60cm) circular needle or size needed to obtain gauge
- Spare needle for BO
- Stitch markers
- Stitch holders and safety pins
- Tapestry needle
- Three ⅝" (1.5cm) buttons (Tip: Buy an extra button and sew it into the side seam, just above the ribbing, to ensure a replacement.)

Gauge

24 sts and 32 rows = 4" (10cm) in St st with larger needles.

27 sts and 37 rows = 4" (10cm) in Chevron pat with larger needles.

Adjust needle size as necessary to obtain correct gauge.

Special Abbreviations

Inc1: Increase 1 st by knitting in front and back of same st.

W&T (Wrap and Turn): Slip next st pwise to RH needle, bring yarn around this st to RS, slip st back to LH needle, bring yarn back to WS, turn work to begin working back in the other direction.

Special Techniques

Chain selvedge: *RS rows:* slip first st, knit last st; *WS rows:* slip first st with yarn in front, purl last st. Work chain selvedge at all edges except neck edges.

Working wrapped sts and wraps tog: Insert RH needle into front of wrap from bottom to top as if to knit, insert RH needle into st itself, knit both the wrap and st tog.

3-needle bind-off: With RS tog and needles parallel, using a 3rd needle, knit tog a st from the front needle with 1 from the back. *Knit tog a st from the front and back needles, and slip the first st over the 2nd to bind off. Rep from * across, leaving last st on holder.

Pattern Notes

• Keep in mind that the tighter your fit, the more it will take up in length, so you may want to add an extra vertical repeat of the stitch pattern before beginning the armhole shaping, and/or extend the waist ribbing, especially if you are tall.

• The back of this sweater is split at the top for a buttonband placket. You could also make a back-button cardigan by working each back half separately and working a longer buttonband from hem to neck, picking up stitches at the rate established.

• Back shoulders are shaped using short rows; front shoulders are not shaped. The shoulder seam will fall to the back.

• In order to organically design the garment shaping around the stitch pattern, there is only 1 size for the armhole shaping and sleeves.

• Markers are helpful when shaping in pattern.

Stitch Pattern

CHEVRON PAT (multiple of 11 sts)
Rows 1, 3, 5, and 7 (RS): *K2tog, k2, Inc1 twice, k3, ssk; rep from * to end.

Rows 2, 4, and 6: Purl.

Rows 8–12: Knit.

Rep Rows 1–12 for pat.

Instructions

BACK
With smaller needles, CO 101 (112, 123) sts.

Row 1 (RS): Sl 1 (selvedge st), *[p1, k1] 5 times, p1; rep from * to last st, k1.

Row 2: Sl 1 (selvedge st) *[k1, p1] 5 times, k1; rep from * to last st, p1.

Rep Rows 1 and 2 until piece measures 2½" (5cm).

With larger needles, establish pat as follows:

Row 1 (RS): Sl 1, work Row 1 of Chevron pat to last st, k1.

Work even in pat, maintaining selvedge sts, until 6 (7, 8) 12-row pat reps are complete.

Work Rows 1–6 of pat once more, placing markers after first 12 sts and before last 12 sts.

Armhole shaping
Maintaining est pat, BO 5 sts at beg of next 2 rows—91 (102, 113) sts.

Dec row (RS): Sl 1, ssk, work to last 3 sts, k2tog, k1—89 (100, 111) sts.

Rep Dec row [every RS row] 4 times, and on pat Rows 1, 3, and 5, work sts outside markers in St st and sts between markers in Chevron pat; on last WS row, remove markers—81 (92, 103) sts.

Next row (RS): Sl 1, k3tog, work in pat to last 4 sts, sssk, k1—79 (90, 101) sts.

Cont in est pat until 10 (11, 12) total reps of Chevron pat are complete (counting from ribbing) and on last RS row of last rep, work 38 (44, 50) sts, Inc1 twice, knit to end—81 (92, 103) sts.

Divide for back neck opening
Sizes S and L only

Next row (RS): Sl 1, work Row 1 of Chevron pat over next 33 (44) sts, k2tog, k2, Inc1, k1 (new selvedge st); join 2nd ball of yarn and k1 (new selvedge st), Inc1, k3, ssk, work Chevron pat over next 33 (44) sts, k1—40 (51) sts right back; 41 (52) sts left back.

Size M only

Next row (RS): Sl 1, work Row 1 of Chevron pat over next 44 sts, k1 (new selvedge st); join 2nd ball of yarn, k1 (new selvedge st), work Chevron pat over next 44 sts, k1—46 sts each side.

All sizes

Working both sides at once with separate balls of yarn, and working the new selvedge sts at split in garter st (k1 on RS and WS), work even until 2 pat reps are complete after splitting back.

Shoulder shaping (short rows)

Rows 1 and 2: Work in pat to neck; work to last 7 (12, 12) sts, W&T.

Rows 3 and 4: Work in pat to neck; work to last 12 (18, 18) sts, W&T.

Rows 5 and 6: Work in pat to neck; work to last 18 (23, 23) sts, W&T.

Rows 7 and 8: Work to end of row, working wrapped sts tog with the wraps as you come to them.

Rows 9 and 10: Work even.

Row 11: Work to center of right back, Inc1 (—, Inc1), work to end—41 (46, 52) sts each side.

Row 12: Work even.

Place 24 (29, 35) sts on holder for shoulder; place 17 sts on holder for back neck; place 17 sts on holder for back neck; place 24 (29, 35) sts on holder for shoulder.

FRONT

With smaller needles, CO 101 (112, 123) sts.

Work as for back until 11 (12, 12) pat reps are complete, omitting division for back neck opening—79 (90, 101) sts.

Front neck shaping
Sizes S and L only

Row 1 (RS): Sl 1, work Row 1 of Chevron pat over next 22 (33) sts, pm, k3, Inc1, k1; place center 21 sts on holder for front neck; join 2nd ball of yarn, k6, pm, work Chevron pat over next 22 (33) sts, k1—29 (40) sts each side.

Row 2 and all WS rows: Working both sides at once with separate balls of yarn, work even in pat.

Rows 3, 5, and 7 (RS): *Left front:* Work in pat to marker, knit to last 4 sts, k2tog, k2; *Right front:* k2, ssk, knit to marker, work in pat to end—26 (37) sts each side.

Rows 9 and 11: Removing markers as you come to them, sl 1, knit to last 4 sts, k2tog, k2; k2, ssk, knit to end—25 (36) sts each side.

Row 12: Work even.

STITCH KEY

☐ K on RS, p on WS

▬ K on WS

╱ K2tog

╲ Ssk

Ƴ K1f&b

■ No stitch

CHEVRON PATTERN

11-st rep

Row 1 (RS): Sl 1, work Row 1 of Chevron pat over next 22 sts, pm, k2tog, k2, Inc1, k6; place center 22 sts on holder for front neck; join a 2nd ball of yarn, k5, Inc1, k3, ssk, pm, work Chevron pat over next 22 sts, k1—34 sts each side.

Row 2 and all WS rows: Working both sides at once with separate balls of yarn, work even in pat.

Row 3: Work in pat to marker, k2tog, k2, Inc1, k2, k2tog, k2; k2, ssk, k1, Inc1, k3, ssk, work in pat to end—33 sts each side.

Row 5: Work in pat to marker, k2tog, k2, Inc1, k1, k2tog, k2; k2, ssk, Inc1, k3, ssk, work in pat to end—32 sts each side.

Row 7: Work in pat to marker, k5, k2tog, k2; k2, ssk, k5, work in pat to end—31 sts each side.

Row 9: Work to last 4 sts, k2tog, k2; k2, ssk, knit to end—30 sts each side.

Rows 11 and 12: Work even.

Next row (all sizes): Sl 1, work in pat to marker, knit to end; knit to marker, work in pat to end.

Work even until 2 (2, 4) more pat reps are complete.

Place sts on holders.

SLEEVES

With smaller needles, CO 79 sts.

Row 1 (RS): Sl 1 (selvedge st), *[p1, k1] 5 times, p1; rep from * to last st, k1.

Row 2: Sl 1 (selvedge st) *[k1, p1] 5 times, k1; rep from * to last st, p1.

Rep Rows 1 and 2 until piece measures 1" (2.5cm).

With larger needles, establish pat and shape sleeve as follows:

Row 1 (RS): Sl 1, Inc1, k3, Inc1 twice, k3, ssk; pm, work Row 1 of Chevron pat over next 55 sts, pm; k2tog, k2, Inc1 twice, k3, Inc1, k2—83 sts.

Row 2 and all WS rows: Work even.

Row 3: Sl 1, Inc1, k5, Inc1 twice, k3, ssk; work in pat between markers; k2tog, k2, Inc1 twice, k5, Inc1, k2—87 sts.

Row 5: Shifting marker positions as indicated, sl 1, Inc1, k3; pm, work Chevron pat over next 77 sts, pm; k2, Inc1, k2—89 sts.

Row 7: Sl 1, Inc1, k4; work in pat between markers; k3, Inc1, k2—91 sts.

Rows 9 and 11: Sl 1, Inc1, knit to last 3 sts, Inc1, k2—95 sts.

Row 13: Sl 1, Inc1, k1, Inc1, k3, ssk; work in pat between markers; k2tog, k2, Inc1, k1, Inc1, k2—97 sts.

Row 15: Sl 1, Inc1, k2, Inc1, k3, ssk; work in pat between markers; k2tog, k2, Inc1, k2, Inc1, k2—99 sts.

Row 17: Sl 1, Inc1, k3, Inc1, k3, ssk; work in pat between markers; k2tog, k2, Inc1, k3, Inc1, k2—101 sts.

Row 18: Work even.

Sleeve cap
Row 19 (RS): BO 6 sts, k5, work Chevron pat over next 88 sts, k1—95 sts.

Row 20: BO 6 sts, knit to last st, p1—89 sts.

Dec row (RS): Sl 1, ssk, work to last 3 sts, k2tog, k1—87 sts.

Rep Dec row [every RS row] 3 times, and on pat Rows 1 and 3, work sts outside markers in St st and sts between markers in Chevron pat; on last WS row, remove markers—81 sts.

Row 29: Shifting markers as indicated, sl 1, k3tog, k2, Inc1 twice, k3, ssk; pm, work Chevron pat over next 55 sts, pm; k2tog, k2, Inc1 twice, k3, sssk, k1—79 sts.

Row 31: Sl 1, work pat over next 77 sts, k1.

Rows 32–36: Work even.

Row 37: Sl 1, ssk, k3, Inc1, k3, ssk; work in pat between markers; k2tog, k2, Inc1, k3, k2tog, k1—77 sts.

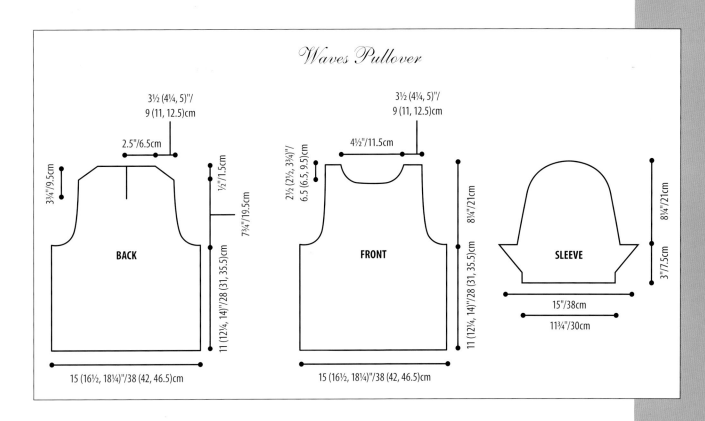

Cont decreasing in this manner [every RS row] 15 times, remembering to work pat incs and decs as pairs when working partial reps to maintain correct st count; if you cannot work both the inc and the dec, work as knit sts—47 sts.

Next row (WS): Sl 1, p2tog, knit to last 3 sts, ssp, p1—45 sts.

Cont in pat, working partial reps on RS rows as knit sts as necessary, dec 1 st at each end of row [every row] 18 times—9 sts.

BO.

Finishing

Weave in ends.

Block pieces to finished measurements.

Starting from armhole edges, join shoulders using 3-needle bind-off.

Put final seam st on safety pin for neckband.

Neckband

With RS facing and using smaller needles, beg at back left neck, work sts on holder as follows: sl 1, [p1, k1] 8 times, pick up and knit 1 st, knit rem st from shoulder seam; pick up and knit 16 (16, 24) sts along front neck edge as follows: [2 sts in each garter st section and 6 sts in Chevron section] 2 (2, 3) times; work front neck sts as follows: [p1, k1] 10 times, p1 (0, 1); pick up and knit 16 (16, 24) sts along front neck edge as before; knit rem st from shoulder seam, pick up and knit 2 sts; work sts on holder as follows: [p1, k1] 10 times—91 (91, 106) sts.

Next row: Sl 1, work in K1, P1 Rib to end.

Work in est rib for 11 more rows.

Using larger needle, BO very loosely in rib.

Buttonhole band

With RS facing and using smaller needles, beg at bottom of left back opening, pick up and knit 29 sts as follows: 1 st in garter st edge, [5 sts in Chevron section, 2 in garter st section] twice, 5 sts in Chevron section, 3 sts in garter st section, 6 sts in selvedge of neckband.

Rows 1 and 3 (WS): Sl 1, *k1, p1; rep from * to end.

Row 2 (RS): Sl 1, *p1, k1; rep from * to end.

Buttonhole row (RS): Sl 1, work 6 sts in rib, yo twice, k2tog, work 5 sts in rib, yo twice, p2tog, work 5 sts in rib, yo twice, k2tog, work in rib to end.

Row 5: Working 1 st in each double yo of previous row, sl 1, work in rib to end—29 sts.

Rows 6–8: Work even.

Using larger needle, BO loosely in rib.

With RS facing, beg at underarm, sew one side of sleeve cap to armhole using mattress st, making sure to align pat on each side and stopping before last garter welt of cap. Sew other side of cap into armhole, then ease top of cap into armhole.

Sew side and sleeve seams, keeping pat aligned.

Weave in all ends.

Sew buttons to right back neck edge.

Pennant Pleated Skirt

Design by Elanor Lynn

This pencil skirt is the classic midcalf-length style that was popular in the early 1950s. The sharp verticality of the pleats creates flattering lines. The skirt is fitted through the waist and hips, easing gently to full width without too much bulk or voluminous knitting by increasing needle size and the number of stitches between repeats.

Sizes

Woman's extra-small (small, medium, large)

Instructions are given for smallest size, with larger sizes in parentheses. When only 1 number is given, it applies to all sizes.

Finished Measurements (at full width)

Waist circumference: 26 (28, 30, 32)"/66 (71, 76, 81.5)cm

Hip circumference: 36 (38¾, 41½, 44¼)"/91.5 (98.5, 105.5, 112.5)cm

Hem circumference: 54½ (58¾, 62 , 67)"/138.5 (149, 157.5, 170)cm

Length: 27½" (70cm)

Materials

- Cascade *220* (worsted weight; 100% wool; 220 yd/100g per skein): 5 (6, 7, 8) skeins charcoal gray #4002
- Size 2 (2.75mm) 24" (60cm) circular needle
- Size 3 (3.25mm) 24" (60cm) circular needle
- Size 4 (3.5mm) 24" (60cm) circular needle
- Size 5 (3.75mm) 24" (60cm) (or longer) circular needle or size needed to obtain gauge
- Stitch markers, 1 in CC for beg of rnd
- Tapestry needle
- 1" (2.5cm)-wide elastic band; length = waist circumference plus 2" (5cm)
- Sewing needle and thread to join elastic

Gauge

28 sts and 36 rnds = 4" (10cm) in St st on smallest needle.

22 sts and 32 rnds = 4" (10cm) in St st on largest needle.

Adjust needle size as necessary to obtain correct gauge.

P1f&b: Purl in front and back of st.

Pattern Notes

• Work with markers! Until you feel confident with the stitch pattern, use stitch markers between every repeat (use a different color to mark the beginning of the round). Instead of purchasing dozens of markers, you can use waste-yarn loops, paper clips, or safety pins.

• This skirt is worked from the top down and is shaped both by increasing stitches and by changing needle sizes incrementally. When directed, change to the next larger needle size, based on your gauge swatches.

• You can easily adapt this pattern for any size by casting on one repeat for every inch around the waist. You can also make it more flared by continuing to increase stitches as established between repeats (buy extra yarn!).

• For an above-the-knee-length skirt, work until 19½" (49.5cm) or shorter. For a really modern version, omit the elastic and wear the waist low. Even though the hem is much fuller than the hips, the pleats allow it to fall so that it appears to be the same width as at the hips. No matter what length you choose, remember to bind off in the middle of the purled pennant point (Rnd 16 of Pattern E) in order to prevent the hem from rolling.

Stitch Patterns

PENNANT PLEATING

Pattern A (7-st rep)
Rnd 1: *P1, k6; rep from * around.

Rnd 2: *P2, k5; rep from * around.

Rnd 3: *P3, k4; rep from * around.

Rnd 4: *P4, k3; rep from * around.

Rnd 5: *P5, k2; rep from * around.

Rnd 6: *P6, k1; rep from * around.

Rnd 7: *P5, k2; rep from * around.

Rnd 8: *P4, k3; rep from * around.

Rnd 9: *P3, k4; rep from * around.

Rnd 10: *P2, k5; rep from * around.

Rnd 11: *P1, k6; rep from * around.

Rnd 12: Knit.

Rep Rnds 1–12 for pat.

Pattern B (8-st rep)
Rnd 1: *P6, k2; rep from * around.

Rnd 2: *P5, k3; rep from * around.

Rnd 3: *P4, k4; rep from * around.

Rnd 4: *P3, k5; rep from * around.

Rnd 5: *P2, k6; rep from * around.

Rnd 6: *P1, k7; rep from * around.

Rnd 7: Knit.

Rnd 8: *P1, k7; rep from * around.

Rnd 9: *P2, k6; rep from * around.

Rnd 10: *P3, k5; rep from * around.

Rnd 11: *P4, k4; rep from * around.

Rnd 12: *P5, k3; rep from * around.

Rnd 13: *P6, k2; rep from * around.

Pattern C (9-st rep)
Rnd 1: *P6, k3; rep from * around.

Rnd 2: *P5, k4; rep from * around.

Rnd 3: *P4, k5; rep from * around.

Rnd 4: *P3, k6; rep from * around.

Rnd 5: *P2, k7; rep from * around.

Rnd 6: *P1, k8; rep from * around.

Rnd 7: Knit.

Rnd 8: *P1, k8; rep from * around.

Rnd 9: *P2, k7; rep from * around.

Rnd 10: *P3, k6; rep from * around.

Rnd 11: *P4, k5; rep from * around.

Rnd 12: *P5, k4; rep from * around.

Rnd 13: *P6, k3; rep from * around.

Pattern D (10-st rep)
Rnd 1: *P6, k4; rep from * around.

Rnd 2: *P5, k5; rep from * around.

Rnd 3: *P4, k6; rep from * around.

Rnd 4: *P3, k7; rep from * around.

Rnd 5: *P2, k8; rep from * around.

Rnd 6: *P1, k9; rep from * around.

Rnd 7: Knit.

Rnd 8: *P1, k9; rep from * around.

Rnd 9: *P2, k8; rep from * around.

Rnd 10: *P3, k7; rep from * around.

Rnd 11: *P4, k6; rep from * around.

Rnd 12: *P5, k5; rep from * around.

Rnd 13: *P6, k4; rep from * around.

Pattern E (11-st rep)

Rnd 1: *P8, k3; rep from * around.

Rnd 2: *P7, k4; rep from * around.

Rnd 3: *P6, k5; rep from * around.

Rnd 4: *P5, k6; rep from * around.

Rnd 5: *P4, k7; rep from * around.

Rnd 6: *P3, k8; rep from * around.

Rnd 7: *P2, k9; rep from * around.

Rnd 8: *P1, k10; rep from * around.

Rnd 9: Knit.

Rnd 10: *P1, k10; rep from * around.

Rnd 11: *P2, k9; rep from * around.

Rnd 12: *P3, k8; rep from * around.

Rnd 13: *P4, k7; rep from * around.

Rnd 14: *P5, k6; rep from * around.

Rnd 15: *P6, k5; rep from * around.

Rnd 16: *P7, k4; rep from * around.

Rep Rnds 1–16 for pat.

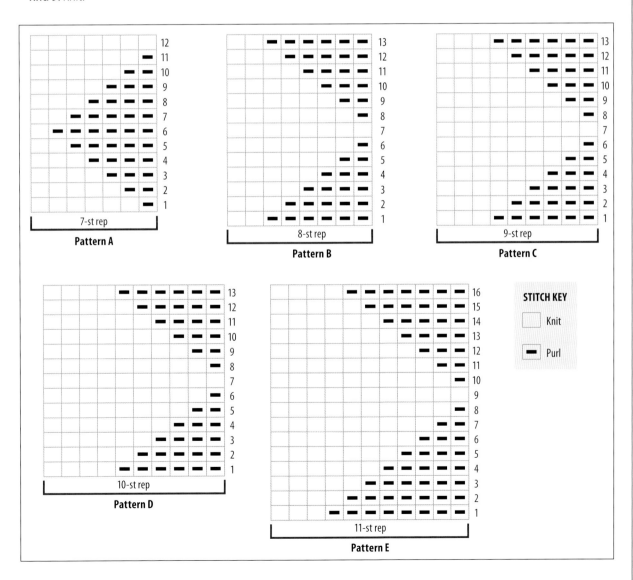

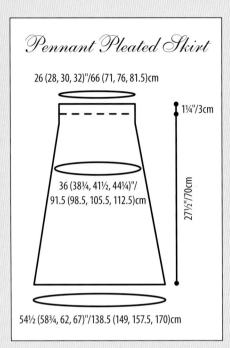

Pennant Pleated Skirt

26 (28, 30, 32)"/66 (71, 76, 81.5)cm

1¼"/3cm

36 (38¾, 41½, 44¼)"/
91.5 (98.5, 105.5, 112.5)cm

27½"/70cm

54½ (58¾, 62, 67)"/138.5 (149, 157.5, 170)cm

Instructions

HEMMED WAISTBAND

With smallest needle and using knit-on method, CO 182 (196, 210, 224) sts; pm for beg of rnd and join, taking care not to twist sts.

Knit 13 rnds.

Turning rnd: Purl.

Knit 12 rnds.

With a spare circular needle, pick up edge loops of cast-on; fold work along turning rnd so that needles are parallel.

Joining rnd: Using the needle in front, *insert right tip into first st on front needle, then into first st on back needle and knit them tog; rep from * around to last 10 sts, k10, dropping the cast-on loops without joining (this is the elastic casing opening).

BODY OF SKIRT

Rnd 1: Cont with smallest needles; *p1, k6, pm; rep from * around.

Next 11 rnds: Work Rnds 2–12 of Pat A.

Next 12 rnds: Change to next larger size needle and work Pat A.

Next 12 rnds: Change to next larger size needle and work Pat A.

Next 18 rnds: Change to largest needle size and work Pat A, ending with Rnd 6.

Inc rnd: *P5, p1f&b, k1; rep from * around—208 (224, 240, 256) sts.

Next 13 rnds: Work Pat B.

Inc rnd: *P5, p1f&b, k2; rep from * around—234 (252, 270, 288) sts.

Next 13 rnds: Work Pat C.

Inc rnd: *P5, p1f&b, k3; rep from * around—260 (280, 300, 320) sts.

Next 13 rnds: Work Pat D.

Inc rnd: *P6, p1f&b, k3; rep from * around—286 (308, 330, 352) sts.

Change to Pat E and work even until piece measures approx 27½" (70cm) from waistband, or desired length, ending with Rnd 16 (16½ purled pennant points).

Bind off *very* loosely in pat (following Rnd 1), using needles approx 3 sizes larger if necessary for elastic edge.

Break yarn.

Finishing

Weave in all ends.

Block to finished measurements.

Insert elastic into casing, overlap ends, and safety-pin together for fitting. Adjust to fit and sew elastic ends together. Sew down 10 cast-on loops to close opening.

Lavender Capelet

Design by Tatyana T. Chambers

This capelet was inspired by the Cobweb Shawl published by Stitchcraft in 1953. Being a modern woman who is always on the go, I prefer to wear something that won't slip off my shoulders or get caught in the car door. A capelet is the answer. Pull it over your head and—voilà—an instant outfit brightener with a touch of sophistication and elegance. Wear it over a T-shirt with jeans while going out for a cup of coffee or on top of an evening dress to keep your shoulders warm when out on the town.

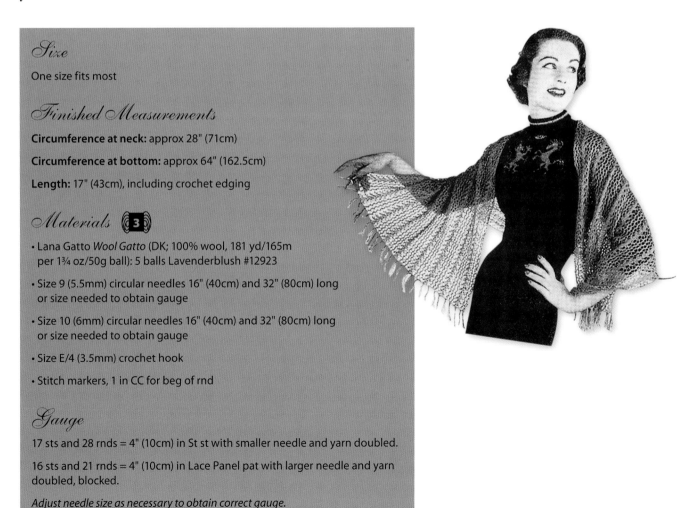

Size
One size fits most

Finished Measurements
Circumference at neck: approx 28" (71cm)

Circumference at bottom: approx 64" (162.5cm)

Length: 17" (43cm), including crochet edging

Materials (3)
• Lana Gatto *Wool Gatto* (DK; 100% wool, 181 yd/165m per 1¾ oz/50g ball): 5 balls Lavenderblush #12923

• Size 9 (5.5mm) circular needles 16" (40cm) and 32" (80cm) long or size needed to obtain gauge

• Size 10 (6mm) circular needles 16" (40cm) and 32" (80cm) long or size needed to obtain gauge

• Size E/4 (3.5mm) crochet hook

• Stitch markers, 1 in CC for beg of rnd

Gauge
17 sts and 28 rnds = 4" (10cm) in St st with smaller needle and yarn doubled.

16 sts and 21 rnds = 4" (10cm) in Lace Panel pat with larger needle and yarn doubled, blocked.

Adjust needle size as necessary to obtain correct gauge.

Slip marker (sm): Slip marker when you come to it.

Make 1 (M1): Insert LH needle from front to back under running thread between st just worked and next st; knit into the resulting loop. Do not twist loop.

Make 1 Purlwise (M1p): Insert RH needle from back to front under the running thread between st just worked and next st and put on LH needle; purl into the resulting loop.

Pattern Notes

• This capelet is worked in the round from the neck down with 2 strands of yarn held together throughout.

• The Lace Panels are 13 stitches and are separated by purl stitches that gradually increase from 1 to 3 stitches.

• For gauge swatch, cast on 29 sts; *RS rows:* work p1, [Lace Panel, p1] twice; *WS rows:* k1, [p13, k1] twice. This stitch pattern will stretch lengthwise by about 25 percent after blocking and is also quite stretchy sideways. Wet-block your gauge swatch accordingly before measuring.

Tip: Since the Lace Panel is worked over only 4 rnds, you might want to mark every 4th round with a contrast-colored thread to remind you where you are in the pattern.

Stitch Pattern

LACE PANEL (13-st panel)
Rnd 1: [K2tog, yo] twice, k1, yo, [k2tog] twice, k2, yo, k2tog, yo.

Rnd 2: K13.

Rnd 3: [Yo, k2tog] twice, yo, k2, [k2tog] twice, yo, k1, yo, k2tog.

Rnd 4: K13.

Rep Rnds 1–4 for pat.

Instructions

With smaller 16" (40cm) needle and 2 strands of yarn held tog and using long-tail method, CO on 90 sts; pm for beg of rnd and join, taking care not to twists sts.

Work 1" (2.5cm) in K1, P1 Rib.

Set-up rnd: *K9, pm; rep from * around.

Inc rnd: *Knit to next marker, M1, sm; rep from * around—100 sts.

Next rnd: Knit.

Inc rnd: *K1, M1, knit to next marker, M1, sm; rep from * around—120 sts.

Next rnd: Knit.

Rep last 2 rnds—140 sts with 14 sts between markers.

Pat set-up rnd: Switch to larger needle; *work Rnd 1 of Lace Panel to 1 st before marker, p1; rep from * around.

Work even in est pat until piece measures approx 10½" (26.5cm), ending with Rnd 2 or 4.

Inc rnd: *Work Lace Panel, M1p, p1, sm; rep from * around—150 sts with 2 purl sts between panels.

Next rnd: Work in est pat, purling new st.

Inc rnd: *Work Lace Panel, p2, M1p, sm; rep from * around—160 sts with 3 purl sts between panels.

Next rnd: Work even in established pat, purling new st.

Work even until piece measures approx 16" (40.5cm) slightly stretched, ending with Rnd 4.

BO very loosely, leaving last st on needle.

CROCHET EDGING

Switch to crochet hook; insert hook into last st, sl st into next st, *ch 4, skip 1 st, sl st into next st, rep from * around, sl st into first st—you will have approx 77 arches around.

Next rnd: *Sc into ch-4 arch, ch 3, sc into same ch-4 arch; rep from * around, sl st into the base of first sc; fasten off.

Weave in ends.

Wet-block to finished measurements.

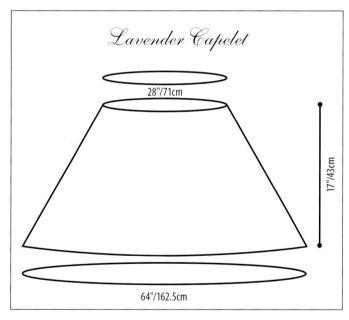

Lavender Capelet

28"/71cm

17"/43cm

64"/162.5cm

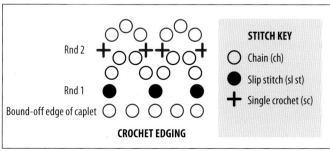

Rnd 2

Rnd 1

Bound-off edge of caplet

STITCH KEY

◯ Chain (ch)

● Slip stitch (sl st)

+ Single crochet (sc)

CROCHET EDGING

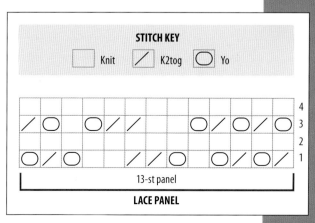

STITCH KEY

| | Knit | ╱ | K2tog | ◯ | Yo |

13-st panel

LACE PANEL

Vintage Lace Socks

Design by Lily M. Chin

These pretty socks are especially fun to knit because the pattern allows you to pick and choose between three classic stitch patterns—rib, lace, and cable—to create your own unique and very vintage socks.

Sizes

To fit woman's shoe size US 6–8 (9–11)/ Euro 36–38.5 (39–42)

Instructions are given for smaller size, with larger size in parentheses. When only 1 number is given, it applies to both sizes.

Finished Measurements

Length from cuff to ankle: 6" (15.5cm)

Foot circumference: 6¾ (8½)"/17 (21.5)cm

Materials

- Lily Chin *Chelsea* (DK weight; 30% merino wool/35% cotton/ 35% acrylic; 191 yd/175m per 1¾ oz/50g ball): 1 (2) balls peach #5803 (see Pattern Notes)

- Size 2 (2.25mm) double-pointed needles (set of 4) or size needed to obtain gauge

- Cable needle (for cabled version)

- Tapestry needle

Gauge

28 sts and 40 rnds = 4" (10cm) in St st.

Adjust needle size as necessary to obtain correct gauge.

Pattern Notes

- This sock is worked from the cuff down with a short-row heel and wedge/decreased toe.

- The knitter has three simple stitch pattern options to choose from for the leg and instep: rib, lace (shown), or cable, each being a multiple of 12 stitches.

- Slip all stitches purlwise.

- Only 1 ball is necessary for small size if leg measures 6" (15cm) as shown in our model. If you choose to make a longer leg, a second ball of yarn may be necessary.

Special Abbreviations

N1, N2, N3: Needle 1, needle 2, needle 3, with N1 holding sole sts and N2 and N3 holding instep sts.

2/1 RC (2 over 1 Right Cross): Sl 1 st to cn and hold in back; k2, k1 from cn.

2/1 LC (2 over 1 Left Cross): Sl 2 sts to cn and hold in front; k1, k2 from cn.

W&T (Wrap and Turn): With yarn held to WS, sl next st pwise to RH needle, bring yarn to RS between needles, slip st back to LH needle, bring yarn back to WS (wrapping slipped st), then turn work to begin working back in the other direction.

WW (Work wrapped sts and wraps tog): *On RS:* Insert RH needle into front of wrap from bottom to top kwise, insert RH needle into st itself, knit both the wrap and st together (it's a little tricky, but wangle the new loop through). *On WS:* With RH needle, pick up wrap from behind and place wrap fully (up and over) onto LH needle—it looks like there are 2 sts on the needle. Purl the wrap and st together.

Stitch Patterns

K1, P1 RIB (even number of sts)
Rnd 1: *K1, p1; rep from * around.

Rep Rnd 1 for pat.

PATTERN #1: RIB (multiple of 12 sts)
Rnd 1: Knit.

Rnd 2: *K2, p2, k6, p2; rep from * around.

Rep Rnds 1 and 2 for pat.

PATTERN #2: LACE (multiple of 12 sts)
Rnd 1: Knit.

Rnd 2: *K2, p2, k1, k2tog, yo, k3, p2; rep from * around.

Rnd 3: Knit.

Rnd 4: *K2, p2, k2tog, yo, k1, yo, ssk, k1, p2; rep from * around.

Rep Rnds 1–4 for pat.

PATTERN #3: CABLE (multiple of 12 sts)
Rnds 1 and 3: Knit.

Rnd 2: *K2, p2, 2/1 RC, 2/1 LC, p2; rep from * around.

Rnd 4: *K2, p2, k6, p2; rep from * around.

Rep Rnds 1–4 for pat.

Instructions

CUFF
CO 48 (60) sts and distribute evenly on 3 dpns; pm for beg of rnd and join, taking care not to twist sts.

Work K1, P1 Rib for 1" (2.5cm).

LEG
Begin desired st pat (rib, lace, or cable) and work even for 6" (15cm) or desired leg length, ending with last rnd of pat and, on last rnd, work until 1 st rem in rnd.

SHORT-ROW HEEL
Arrange the sts on 3 dpns with next 22 (28) sts on N1 for heel and 13 (16) sts each on N2 and N3 for instep. (Note: The first heel st is the st that was the last st of previous rnd—this will balance the instep pattern.)

Row 1 (RS): Knit to last st on N1, W&T.

Row 2: Purl to last st, W&T.

Row 3: Knit to st before previously wrapped st (i.e. 2 sts holding on LH needle), W&T.

Row 4: Purl to st before previously wrapped st, W&T.

Rep [Rows 3 and 4] 5 (7) more times, working 1 fewer st each row before wrap—7 (9) wrapped sts at each end.

Next row (RS): K8 (10) to first wrapped st; WW 7 (9) sts; wrap first st on N2, slip wrapped st back to N2; turn.

Next row: Purl to first wrapped st; WW 7 (9) sts; wrap first st on N3, slip wrapped st back to N3; turn.

Row 1 (RS): K15 (19), W&T.

Row 2: P8 (10), W&T.

Row 3: Knit to wrapped st, WW, W&T.

Row 4: Purl to wrapped st, WW, W&T.

Rep [Rows 3 and 4] 5 (7) more times (working 1 more st each row), until last st on needle has been wrapped.

FOOT

Rnd 1: N1 (sole sts): knit to last st, WW; N2: WW, work in est pat to end; N3: work in est pat to last st, WW by lifting wrap over st onto left needle, then ssk-ing them tog.

Rnd 2: N1: WW with ssk, knit to end; N2 and N3: work in est pat.

Continue working sole sts in St st and instep sts in est pat until foot measures approx 7½ (8¼)"/19 (21)cm or 2" (5cm) short of desired length; if trying on sock, foot should end at small toe.

TOE

N1 and N2: knit across. N3 is now beg of rnd and will be deemed N1 from now on.

Rnd 1: N1: knit to last 3 sts, k2tog, k1; N2: k1, ssk, knit to last 3 sts, k2tog, k1; N3: k1, ssk to dec, knit to end.

Rnd 2: Knit around.

Rep Rnds 1 and 2 until 16 (20) sts rem, ending with Rnd 1.

Knit 4 (5) sts from N1 onto N3.

Cut yarn, leaving a 16" (40.5cm) tail.

With RS facing with needles parallel, using tail and tapestry needle, graft sts using Kitchener st.

Or, if you prefer, turn sock inside out and work 3-needle bind-off.

Weave in tails. Block to finished measurements.

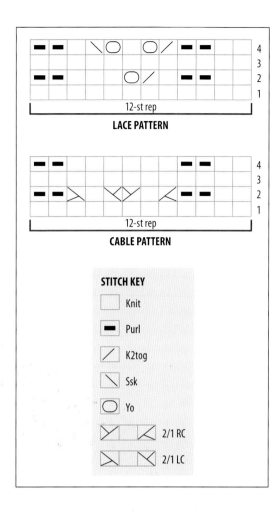

LACE PATTERN

CABLE PATTERN

STITCH KEY

☐	Knit
▬	Purl
╱	K2tog
╲	Ssk
◯	Yo
	2/1 RC
	2/1 LC

Nordic Pullover

Design by Kristin Spurkland

Inspired by photos of women's Norwegian sweaters from the 1940s, this sweater incorporates a "retro" fit (deep ribbing at the lower hem, a short waist, and a close fit in the shoulders and armholes). The colors are meant to evoke vintage style while still feeling contemporary and completely modern.

Sizes

Woman's small (medium, large, extra-large)

Instructions are given for smallest size, with larger sizes in parentheses. When only 1 number is given, it applies to all sizes.

Finished Measurements

Circumference: 36 (41, 44½, 50)"/90.5 (103.5, 112, 127)cm

Length to shoulders: 20 (21½, 23, 24½)"/ 50.5 (54, 58, 62)cm

Materials

- Jamieson's *Shetland Spindrift* (fingering weight; 100% Shetland wool; 115 yd/105m per 25g ball): 8 (10, 11, 13) balls Grouse #235 (MC); 1 (1, 1, 2) balls each Sorbet #570 (A) and Rose #550 (B)

- Size 2 (2.25mm) straight and 16" (40cm) circular needles

- Size 3 (3.25mm) needles or size needed to obtain gauge

- Stitch holders or waste yarn

- Tapestry needle

Gauge

28 sts and 36 rows = 4" (10cm) in stranded St st with larger needles (washed and blocked).

Adjust needle size as necessary to obtain correct gauge.

Special Abbreviations

M1L (Make 1 Left): Insert LH needle from front to back under the running thread between the last st worked and next st on LH needle; knit into the back of resulting loop.

M1R (Make 1 Right): Insert LH needle from back to front under the running thread between the last st worked and next st on LH needle. With RH needle, knit into the front of resulting loop.

Pattern Notes

- Gauge may change significantly upon blocking. For best fit, wash gauge swatch and check gauge after drying.

- The suggested ease of this garment is +2" (5cm).

- Yarns A and B can be carried up the side of the work when not in use or broken at each color change and woven in later.

- Work pattern repeats into shaping. The designer opted to eliminate patterning at the beginning/end of rows where there weren't enough stitches for a complete pattern repeat; you may work partial repeats if desired.

Instructions

BACK
With smaller needles and MC, CO 127 (145, 157, 175) sts.

Row 1 (WS): P2, *k1, p1; rep from * to last st, p1.

Row 2 (RS): K2, *p1, k1; rep from * to last st, k1.

Work even in est rib until piece measures 3" (7.5cm), ending with a RS row.

Change to larger needles and St st; following Chart, work even until piece measures 12 (13, 14, 14½)", ending with a WS row.

Armhole shaping
Cont in est pat and BO 6 sts at beg of next 2 rows—115 (133, 145, 163) sts.

BO 2 sts at beg of next 6 (6, 8, 10) rows—103 (121, 129, 143) sts.

Dec row (RS): K1, ssk, work in pat to last 3 sts, k2tog, k1—101 (119, 127, 141) sts.

Rep Dec row [every RS row] 7 (11, 12, 15) times—87 (97, 103, 111) sts.

Work even until armhole measures 8 (8½, 9, 10)", ending with a WS row.

Neck and shoulder shaping
Row 1 (RS): BO 5 (6, 6, 7) sts [1 st rem on right needle from BO], work 18 (20, 21, 22) sts, slip center 39 (43, 47, 51) sts to holder for back neck, join new ball and work to end of row.

Working both sides at once with 2 balls of yarn, cont in pat as follows:

Row 2: BO 5 (6, 6, 7) sts, work to end—19 (21, 22, 23) sts each side.

Row 3: BO 5 (6, 6, 7) sts, work to 3 sts before neck edge, k2tog, k1; k1, ssk, work to end.

Row 4: BO 5 (6, 6, 7) sts, work to end—13 (14, 15, 15) sts each side.

Row 5: BO 6 (6, 7, 7) sts, work to 3 sts before neck edge, k2tog, k1; k1, ssk, work to end.

Row 6: BO 6 (6, 7, 7) sts, work to end—6 (7, 7, 7) sts each side.

Row 7: BO 6 (7, 7, 7) sts; work to end.

Row 8: BO 6 (7, 7, 7) sts.

FRONT
Work as for back until armhole measures 5 (5½, 6, 7)"/12.5 (14, 15, 18)cm, ending with a WS row.

Neck shaping
Work 36 (40, 42, 45) sts, slip center 15 (17, 19, 21) sts to holder for front neck, join new ball and work to end of row.

Working both sides at once with 2 balls of yarn, cont in pat as follows:

Next 8 (8, 10) rows: BO 2 sts at each neck edge 4 (4, 5, 5) times per side—28 (32, 32, 35) sts each side.

Dec row (RS): Work to 3 sts before neck edge, k2tog, k1; k1, ssk, work to end—27 (31, 31, 34) sts each side.

Rep Dec row [every RS row] 5 (6, 5, 6) times—22 (25, 26, 28) sts each side.

Work even until armhole measures 8 (8½, 9, 10)", ending with a WS row.

Shoulder shaping
BO 5 (6, 6, 7) sts at beg of next 4 (6, 4, 8) rows.

BO 6 (7, 7) sts at beg of next 4 (1, 4, 0) rows.

SLEEVES
With smaller needles and MC, CO 79 (85, 91, 103) sts.

Row 1 (WS): P2, *k1, p1; rep from * to last st, p1.

Row 2: K2, *p1, k1; rep from * to last st, k1.

Work even in est rib until piece measures 1" (2.5cm), ending with a RS row.

Next row (WS): Change to larger needles and St st; beg working Chart.

Inc row (RS): K1, M1R, work in pat to last st, M1L, k1—81 (87, 93, 105) sts.

Cont working Chart and rep Inc row [every 6 rows] 4 more times—89 (95, 101, 113) sts.

Work even until piece measures 4" (10cm), ending with a WS row.

Sleeve cap
BO 6 sts at beg of next 2 rows—77 (83, 89, 101) sts.

BO 2 sts at beg of next 6 (6, 8, 10) rows—65 (71, 73, 81) sts.

Dec row (RS): K1, ssk, work to last 3 sts, k2tog, k1—63 (69, 71, 79) sts.

Rep Dec row [every RS row] 15 (18, 18, 22) times—33 (33, 35, 35) sts.

BO 3 (3, 2, 2) sts at beg of next 4 (4, 2, 2) rows, then 0 (0, 3, 3) sts at beg of following 0 (0, 2, 2) rows—21 (21, 25, 25) sts.

BO rem sts.

Finishing

Weave in all ends.

Block pieces to finished measurements.

Sew shoulder seams. Sew in sleeves. Sew sleeve and side seams.

Neckband
With smaller circular needle and MC, pick up and knit 122 (128, 134, 140) sts evenly around neck.

Work in K1, P1 Rib for 1" (2.5cm).

BO in loosely in rib.

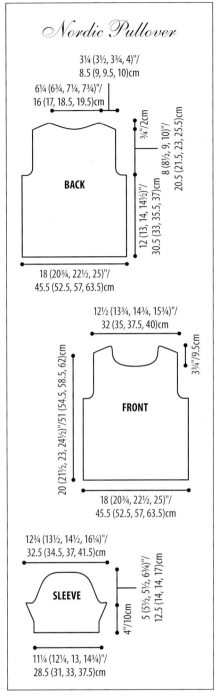

Nordic Pullover

3¼ (3½, 3¾, 4)"/
8.5 (9, 9.5, 10)cm

6¼ (6¾, 7¼, 7¾)"/
16 (17, 18.5, 19.5)cm

¾"/2cm

8 (8½, 9, 10)"/
20.5 (21.5, 23, 25.5)cm

BACK

12 (13, 14, 14½)"/
30.5 (33, 35.5, 37)cm

18 (20¾, 22½, 25)"/
45.5 (52.5, 57, 63.5)cm

12½ (13¾, 14¾, 15¾)"/
32 (35, 37.5, 40)cm

3¾"/9.5cm

FRONT

20 (21½, 23, 24½)"/51 (54.5, 58.5, 62)cm

18 (20¾, 22½, 25)"/
45.5 (52.5, 57, 63.5)cm

12¾ (13½, 14½, 16¼)"/
32.5 (34.5, 37, 41.5)cm

5 (5½, 5½, 6¾)"/
12.5 (14, 14, 17)cm

SLEEVE

4"/10cm

11¼ (12¼, 13, 14¾)"/
28.5 (31, 33, 37.5)cm

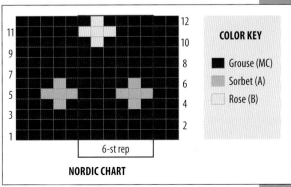

COLOR KEY

■ Grouse (MC)

■ Sorbet (A)

□ Rose (B)

6-st rep

NORDIC CHART

Jacqueline Bouvier Stole

Design by Franklin Habit

Inspired by the veil and dress Jacqueline Bouvier wore on her wedding day, this breathtaking stole is a lacy homage to one of the great style icons of the twentieth century. This design shares the same keynotes of romance, freshness, abundance, and elegance of the postwar "New Look" that Miss Bouvier so eloquently set forth.

Finished Measurements

15 x 80" (38 x 203cm)

Materials

• Lorna's Laces *Helen's Lace* (lace weight; 50% wool/50% silk; 1,250 yd/1,143m per 4 oz/113g skein): 1 skein Natural

• Size 3 (3.25mm) needles or size needed to obtain gauge

• Small tapestry needle

Gauge

22 sts and 32 rows = 4" (10cm) in St st (firmly blocked).

Adjust needle size as necessary to obtain correct gauge.

- The stole is knit flat in 2 halves, which are then grafted together using Kitchener stitch.

- The first and last 4 stitches of the stole are an edging; they are not included in the charts.

- Cast on very loosely by casting on over 2 needles held together or by using a needle 2 sizes larger than main needle.

- The charts show the right-side rows only; purl all wrong-side rows.

- The use of 2 different left-leaning decreases (skp and ssk) is deliberate; sometimes the raised stitch of the former is desirable, and at other times the less obtrusive appearance of the latter is preferable.

- To give the eyelets a neater appearance, I like working a k1-tbl on the first right-side row after working a yarnover. Although not all the yarnovers were worked this way (deliberately!), those that were are marked on the chart.

- The chart has heavier rules every 5 stitches to help the knitter count long stretches of knit stitches more easily.

Stitch Pattern

EDGING
(4 sts, worked at beg and end each row)
Row 1 (RS): *Beg of row:* Yo, p2tog, k2; *end of row:* k3, k1-tbl.

Row 2: *Beg of row:* Yo, k2tog, p2; *end of row:* p3, k1.

Rep Rows 1 and 2 for pat.

BORDER AND BODY PATTERNS (83 sts)
See Charts.

Instructions

FIRST HALF
Loosely CO 91 sts.

Set-up row (RS): Work 4 sts in Edging pat, work Row 1 of Chart 1 (Border) over the next 83 sts, work 4 sts in Edging pat.

Working 4-st Edging pat on all rows, continue working Border chart through Row 45, ending after completing a WS row.

Work Chart 2 (Body) twice, then work Rows 1–45 of Body Chart once more, ending after completing a WS row.

Do not bind off; cut yarn, leaving a 6" (15cm) tail, and place live sts on holder or waste yarn.

SECOND HALF
Work as for first half, but leave live sts on needle in preparation for grafting.

Cut yarn, leaving a generous tail, approx 60" (152cm) long, for grafting.

FINISHING
Transfer first-half sts back to separate needle.

With RS facing and needles parallel, and leaving a 6" (15cm) tail to begin, graft halves together using Kitchener stitch. When grafting is complete, cut yarn, leaving a 6" (15cm) tail for weaving in *after blocking*. Lay the piece on a flat work surface and gently adjust tension of the grafted row to match the rest of the piece.

Soak finished stole thoroughly and, with WS up, block firmly, shaping top and bottom edges into scallops as shown in photograph and pinnning out the loops of the right and left edges. Allow to dry completely. Before removing blocking pins or wires, carefully weave in all loose ends.

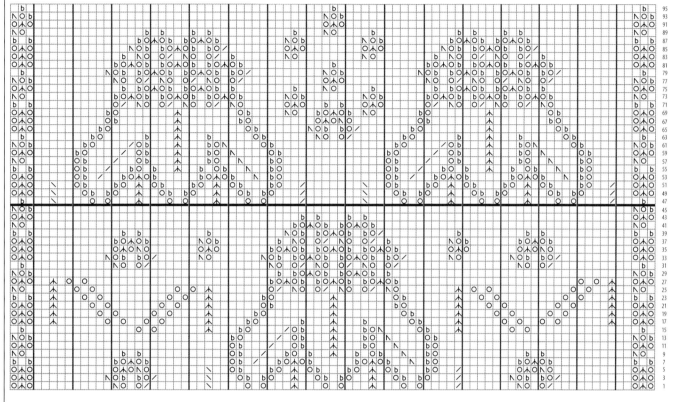

CHART 2: BODY

End last rep here.

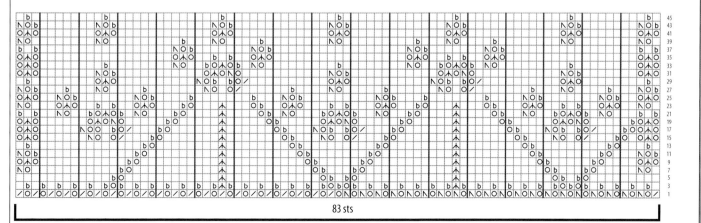

83 sts

CHART 1: BORDER

59

Classic Cloche

Design by Annie Modesitt

A deep-crowned cloche looks good on many heads, flatters many faces, and adds an air of literary mystery to any woman's life. It's perfect for strolls along the beach, but don't wear it into the ocean.

Sizes

To fit head size 18 (20, 22, 24)"/45.5 (51, 56, 61)cm

Instructions are given for smallest size, with larger sizes in parentheses. When only 1 number is given, it applies to all sizes.

Materials

• Hand Maiden *Casbah Sock* (sport weight; 81% merino wool/9% cashmere/10% nylon; 356 yd/325m per 4 oz/115g skein): 1 skein Peridot

• Size 5 (3.75mm) double-pointed and 24" (60cm) circular needles or size needed to obtain gauge

• Size F/5 (3.75mm) crochet hook

• Stitch markers, 1 in CC for beg of rnd

• Tapestry needle

• Heavyweight/button thread

• 3 yd (3m) #18 gauge millinery wire (available at millinery supply houses or online at www.judithm.com)

Gauge

24 sts and 30 rnds = 4" (10cm) in lace pat (see *Pattern Notes*).

Adjust needle size as necessary to obtain correct gauge.

Sssk: Sl 3 sts knitwise 1 at a time, then k3tog from this position; a left-leaning double dec.

S2KP2: Sl 2 sts as if to k2tog, k1, pass slipped sts over; a vertical double dec.

S3KP3: Sl 3 sts as if to k3tog, ssk, pass slipped sts over; a vertical quad dec.

Pattern Notes

• Work gauge swatch by repeating Rnds 3 and 4 of Crown.

• The brim is worked from the inside to the outer rim. Crown stitches are picked up from the inner brim.

• Change to double-pointed needles when stitches no longer fit comfortably on the circular needle.

• When using millinery wire, it is necessary to "spring" the wire when working in large circumferences (wide hat brims). Springing the wire simply means drawing it between your thumb and forefinger to straighten the natural curve, or spring, in the wire. When springing the wire, be careful to move your thumb *slowly* over the wire; move too fast, and you'll give yourself a nasty "wire burn"!

Instructions

BRIM
CO 108 (120, 132, 144) sts; do not join.

Rows 1 (WS) and 2: Knit.

Pm for beg of rnd and join, taking care not to twist the sts.

Rnd 1: *[K1, yo] twice, k1, S3KP3, [k1, yo] twice, k2; rep from * around.

Rnd 2 and all even rnds, unless specified: Knit.

Rnd 3: *K1, yo, k3, S2KP2, [yo, k1] twice; rep from * around.

Rnd 5: *K1, yo, k3, S2KP2, [yo, k1] twice, yo; rep from * around—126 (140, 154, 168) sts.

Rnd 7: *K5, sl 1, k5, yo, k3, yo; rep from * around—144 (160, 176, 192) sts.

Rnd 9: *K5, sl 1, k5, yo, k5, yo; rep from * around—162 (180, 198, 216) sts.

Rnd 11: *K5, sl 1, k5, yo, k7, yo; rep from * around—180 (200, 220, 240) sts.

Rnd 13: Knit.

Rnd 14: Purl.

Rnd 15: *K2tog, yo; rep from * around.

Rnd 16: Purl.

Rnd 17: Knit.

Picot BO: BO loosely as follows: *ssk, slip st just created back onto left needle, knit this st, slip st just created back onto LH needle; rep from * around, creating an extra "picot" st between each bound-off st.

Using the tail from the cast-on, sew edges of first 2 rows tog to close cast-on circle.

CROWN
Pick up and knit 13 sts for each 12-st section of Row 1 of brim as follows: *Pick up and knit 6 sts, yo, pick up and knit 6 sts; rep from * around, pm for beg of rnd—117 (130, 143, 156) sts.

Rnd 1: *K2tog, yo; rep from * until 1 (0, 1, 0) st rem, k1 (—, k1, —).

Rnd 2: Purl.

Rnd 3: *K3tog, k2, [yo, k1] 4 times, k1, sssk; rep from * around.

Rnd 4: Knit.

Rep [Rnds 3 and 4] 0 (1, 2, 2) times more.

Note: In smaller sizes, Rnds 5, 6, and/or 7, 8 are omitted.

Rnd 9: Purl.

Rnd 10: Rep Rnd 1.

Rnd 11: Purl.

Rnds 12 and 13: Knit.

Rnds 14–16: Rep Rnds 9–11.

Rep Rnds 3–16 as worked for your size 0 (0, 1, 1) times.

Rep Rnds 3–16 once more.

If you would like a deeper crown, rep Rnds 3 and 4 until desired crown depth is reached.

TOP
Rnd 1: *K3tog, k3, yo, k1, yo, k3, sssk; rep from * around—99 (110, 121, 132) sts.

Rnd 2 and all even rnds: Knit.

Rnd 3: *K2tog, k3, yo, k1, yo, k3, ssk; rep from * around.

Rep [Rnds 3 and 4] 3 (4, 5, 5) times.

Rnd 5: *K2tog, k1, yo, k1, S2KP2, k1, yo, k1, ssk; rep from * around—81 (90, 99, 108) sts.

Rnd 7: *K2tog, k1, yo, S2KP2, yo, k1, ssk; rep from * around—63 (70, 77, 84) sts.

Rnd 9: *K2tog, yo, S2KP2, yo, ssk; rep from * around—45 (50, 55, 60) sts.

Rnd 11: *K1, S2KP2, k1; rep from * around—27 (30, 33, 36) sts.

Rnd 13: S2KP2 around—9 (10, 11, 12) sts.

Break yarn, leaving an 8" (20cm) tail; using tapestry needle, thread tail through rem sts and pull tight.

Finishing

Weave in ends.

Steam block the brim with an iron, very lightly pressing the wrong side of the brim. Lay the hat on a flat surface (tabletop or floor).

Create wire rim
Spring the milliner's wire (see Pattern Notes). Make a slip knot in the end of an 18" (45.5cm) strand of heavyweight thread and tighten the knot around the end of the wire.

Lay the sprung milliner's wire around the outer edge of the brim so that the circumference of the wire is about 1" (2.5cm) larger than the circumference of the hat brim. Without cutting the wire, temporarily tape the wire circle closed at this point.

Begin doubling the rim wire by working the excess wire around the established circumference and wrapping both thicknesses of wire together with the heavy thread. Wraps should be about ⅛" (.3cm) apart and should be rather tight. Continue working around the brim wire, adding to the heavy thread as necessary by tying on new 18" (45.5cm) pieces (the knots will be covered when the hat is attached to the wire rim). Work until the entire rim wire is doubled, then work 1" (2.5cm) beyond the taped area (removing tape as you work past that part).

Cut the wire. Wrap the heavy thread very tightly around the doubled ends of the wire, making sure to cover the cut ends as thoroughly as possible, but do not create a bulky bump. Secure the thread by knotting it around the wire, then weaving it back under the wrapped strands. Working back around the brim, weave all thread ends into the wrapped strands in the same manner.

Join wire to brim
Using a strand of project yarn, make a loop on the crochet hook by pulling the strand through a st on the outer edge of the brim. Rest the wire circle on top of the brim and hold it gently in the same hand along with the brim.

*Working beneath the wire, push the crochet hook through the next st along the brim edge. Continuing to work beneath the wire, pull a loop of the yarn back through the 2nd st so that there are 2 loops on the crochet hook. Working above the wire, pull a strand of yarn through both sts on the crochet hook. Rep from * around. (In order to completely cover the brim wire, and depending on the thickness of the yarn, it may be necessary to work more than one crochet st into each knit st along the brim edge.)

The brim should attach to the wire tautly; it may be necessary to pull on the fabric as the attachment of the wire to the brim nears completion to even out the brim fabric around the entire wire.

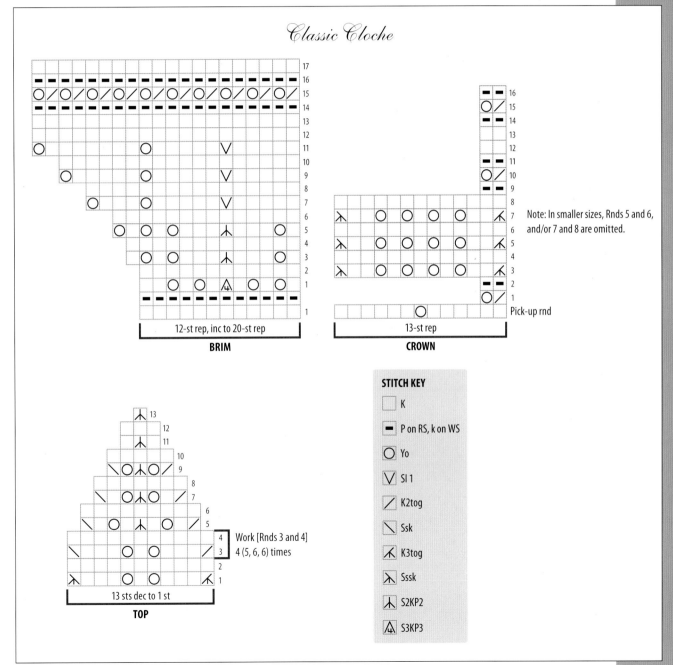

Classic Cloche

BRIM
12-st rep, inc to 20-st rep

CROWN
13-st rep

Note: In smaller sizes, Rnds 5 and 6, and/or 7 and 8 are omitted.

TOP
13 sts dec to 1 st

Work [Rnds 3 and 4] 4 (5, 6, 6) times

STITCH KEY

☐	K
▬	P on RS, k on WS
O	Yo
V	Sl 1
╱	K2tog
╲	Ssk
⋏	K3tog
⋏	Sssk
⋏	S2KP2
⋀	S3KP3

Diamond Vest with Bow

Design by Melissa Wehrle

An old diamond pattern gets new life when placed on a modern fitted vest. The grosgrain ribbon and bow on the placket add a little bit of vintage charm and interest.

Sizes

To fit bust size 30 (34, 37, 40, 44, 48, 52)"/76 (86.5, 94, 101.5, 122, 132)cm

Instructions are given for smallest size, with larger sizes in parentheses. When only 1 number is given, it applies to all sizes.

Finished Measurements

Chest: 30 (34, 37, 40, 44, 48, 52)"/76 (86.5, 94, 101.5, 122, 132)cm

Length: 21½ (22, 22½, 23½, 24, 24½, 25)"/54.5 (56, 57, 59.5, 61, 62, 63.5)cm

Materials

- Rowan *Wool Cotton* (DK weight; 50% merino wool/50% cotton; 123 yd/134.5m per 1¾ oz/50g ball): 5 (5, 6, 7, 7, 8, 9) balls Smalt #SH963

- Size 5 (3.75mm) straight needles or size needed to obtain gauge

- Size 4 (3.5mm) straight and 16" (40cm) circular needle

- Stitch marker

- Tapestry needle

- 2 yd (2m) grosgrain ribbon ¾" (2cm) wide

- 5 (5, 5, 5, 5, 6, 6) ⅝" (1.5cm) buttons

- Sewing needle and matching thread

Gauge

21 sts and 32 rows = 4" (10cm) in Diamond pat with larger needles.

24 sts and 32 rows = 4" (10cm) in K2, P2 Rib with smaller needles.

Adjust needle size as necessary to obtain correct gauge.

1-row, 4-st buttonhole: Yarn forward, sl 1, yarn back, [slip 1, BO 1] 4 times, sl last bind-off st from the RH needle back to the LH needle. Turn work and, using cable CO method, CO 5 sts, turn work and sl the first st on the LH needle over to the RH needle and pass the extra cast-on st on the RH needle over to close the buttonhole.

Pattern Notes

• This pattern assumes no ease for very close fit.

• Read pattern through carefully before beginning. Front neck shaping is worked at the same time as waist and armhole shaping.

• Be careful not to bind off ribbed placket and neck stitches too tightly; if necessary, go up one needle size for the bind-off.

Stitch Pattern

DIAMOND PATTERN
(multiple of 8 sts + 9)

Row 1 (RS): K4, *p1, k7; rep from * to last 5 sts, p1, k4.

Row 2: P3, *k1, p1, k1, p5; rep from * to last 6 sts, k1, p1, k1, p3.

Row 3: K2, *p1, k3; rep from * to last 3 sts, p1, k2.

Row 4: P1, *k1, p5, k1, p1; rep from * to end.

Row 5: *P1, k7; rep from * to last st, p1.

Row 6: Rep Row 4.

Row 7: Rep Row 3.

Row 8: Rep Row 2.

Rep Rows 1–8 for pat.

Instructions

BACK

With smaller needles, CO 86 (98, 106, 114, 126, 138, 150) sts.

Row 1 (RS): K2, *p2, k2; rep from * to end.

Cont in est K2, P2 Rib until piece measures 2" (5cm), ending with a RS row. Change to larger needles.

Dec row (WS): P11 (8, 7, 15, 9, 12, 7), [p2tog, k13 (8, 9, 9, 7, 12, 9)] 5 (9, 9, 9, 13, 9, 13) times—81 (89, 97, 105, 113, 129, 137) sts.

Waist shaping

Beg working Diamond pat and work 2 rows even.

Dec row (RS): K1, ssk, work in pat to last 3 sts, k2tog, k1—79 (87, 95, 103, 111, 127, 135) sts.

Rep Dec row [every 6 (8, 8, 8, 10, 6, 8) rows] 5 (4, 4, 3, 1, 6, 1) time(s), then [every 0 (0, 0, 10, 12, 0, 10) rows] 0 (0, 0, 1, 2, 0, 3) times—69 (79, 87, 95, 105, 115, 127) sts.

Work 7 rows even.

Inc row (RS): K1, M1, work in pat to last st, M1, k1—71 (81, 89, 97, 107, 117, 129) sts.

Rep Inc row [every 10 (10, 10, 10, 10, 8, 10) rows] 4 (3, 3, 2, 1, 2, 2) times, then [every 0 (12, 12, 12, 12, 10, 12) rows] 0 (1, 1, 2, 3, 3, 3) times, working new sts into pat—79 (89, 97, 105, 115, 127, 137) sts.

Work even until back measures 13¼ (13¾, 13¾, 14¼, 14½, 14¾, 14¾)", ending with a WS row.

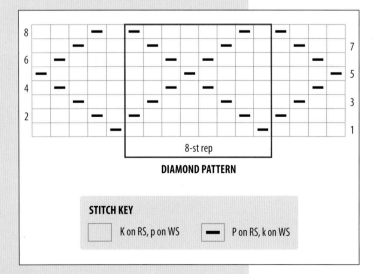

DIAMOND PATTERN

8-st rep

STITCH KEY

☐ K on RS, p on WS   ▬ P on RS, k on WS

Armhole shaping

BO 7 (7, 8, 8, 11, 11, 12) sts at beg of the next 2 rows—65 (75, 81, 89, 93, 105, 113) sts.

Dec 1 st at each end [every row] 3 (5, 5, 5, 7, 9, 9) times, then [every RS row] 3 (4, 4, 5, 4, 5, 7) times—53 (57, 63, 69, 71, 77, 81) sts.

Work even until armhole measures 7¾ (7¾, 8¼, 8¾, 9, 9¼, 9¾)", ending with a WS row.

Back neck and shoulder shaping

Mark center 35 (37, 37, 41, 43, 43, 45) sts for back neck.

Row 1 (RS): BO 4 (4, 6, 6, 6, 8, 8) sts, work in pat to marked back neck; join a 2nd ball of yarn and BO center 35 (37, 37, 41, 43, 43, 45) sts, work to end of row.

Row 2: Working both sides at once with separate balls of yarn, BO 4 (4, 6, 6, 6, 8, 8) sts, work to neck; ssp, work to end of row.

Row 3: BO rem 4 (5, 6, 7, 7, 8, 9) sts to neck; k2tog, work to end of row.

Row 4: BO rem 4 (5, 6, 7, 7, 8, 9) sts.

LEFT FRONT

With smaller needles, CO 38 (46, 50, 54, 62, 66, 74) sts.

Work in rib as for Back, ending with a RS row.

Change to larger needles.

Dec row (WS): P10 (6, 5, 4, 6, 11, 4) [p2tog, k12 (6, 7, 8, 6, 9, 8)] 2 (5, 5, 5, 7, 5, 7) times—36 (41, 45, 49, 55, 61, 67) sts.

Waist shaping

Beg working Diamond pat and work 2 rows even.

Dec row (RS): K1, ssk, work to end—35 (40, 44, 48, 54, 60, 66) sts.

Rep Dec row [every 6 (8, 8, 8, 10, 6, 8) rows] 5 (4, 4, 3, 1, 6, 1) time(s), then [every 0 (0, 0, 10, 12, 0, 10) rows] 0 (0, 0, 1, 2, 0, 3) time(s)—30 (36, 40, 44, 51, 54, 62) sts.

Work 7 rows even.

Inc Row (RS): K1, M1, work to end of row—31 (37, 41, 45, 52, 55, 63) sts.

Rep Inc Row [every 10 (10, 10, 10, 10, 8, 10) rows] 4 (3, 3, 2, 1, 2, 2) time(s), then [every 0 (12, 12, 12, 12, 10, 12) rows] 0 (1, 1, 2, 3, 3, 3) time(s), working new sts into pat—35 (41, 45, 49, 56, 60, 68) sts.

Work side edge even until piece measures 13¼ (13¾, 13¾, 14¼, 14½, 14¾, 14¾)", ending with a WS row, then go to Armhole shaping.

Front neck shaping

At the same time, when piece measures 9¾ (10, 10¼, 11, 11¼, 11½, 11¾)", ending with a WS row, start neck shaping as follows:

Neck dec row (RS): Work to last 2 sts, k2tog.

Rep Neck dec row at neck edge [every 6 (4, 6, 4, 4, 4, 4) rows] 9 (1, 15, 5, 13, 6, 14) times, then [every 8 (6, 0, 6, 6, 6, 6) rows] 4 (14, 0, 12, 7, 12, 7) times.

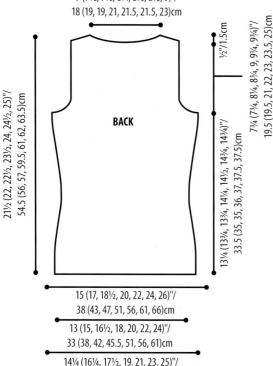

Diamond Vest with Bow

BACK

7 (7½, 7½, 8¼, 8½, 8½, 9)"/
18 (19, 19, 21, 21.5, 21.5, 23)cm

½"/1.5cm

7¾ (7¾, 8¼, 8¾, 9, 9¼, 9¾)"/
19.5 (19.5, 21, 22, 23, 23.5, 25)cm

13¼ (13¾, 13¾, 14¼, 14½, 14¾, 14¾)"/
33.5 (35, 35, 36, 37, 37.5, 37.5)cm

21½ (22, 22½, 23½, 24, 24½, 25)"/
54.5 (56, 57, 59.5, 61, 62, 63.5)cm

15 (17, 18½, 20, 22, 24, 26)"/
38 (43, 47, 51, 56, 61, 66)cm

13 (15, 16½, 18, 20, 22, 24)"/
33 (38, 42, 45.5, 51, 56, 61)cm

14¼ (16¼, 17½, 19, 21, 23, 25)"/
36 (41.5, 44.5, 48.5, 53.5, 58.5, 63.5)cm

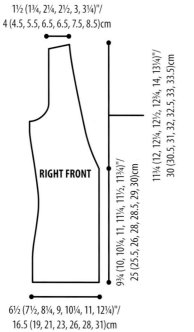

RIGHT FRONT

1½ (1¾, 2¼, 2½, 3, 3¼)"/
4 (4.5, 5.5, 6.5, 6.5, 7.5, 8.5)cm

11¾ (12, 12¼, 12½, 12¾, 14, 13¼)"/
30 (30.5, 31, 32, 32.5, 33, 33.5)cm

9¾ (10, 10¼, 11, 11¼, 11½, 11¾)"/
25 (25.5, 26, 28, 28.5, 29, 30)cm

6½ (7½, 8¼, 9, 10¼, 11, 12¼)"/
16.5 (19, 21, 23, 26, 28, 31)cm

Armhole shaping
Next row (RS): BO 7 (7, 8, 8, 11, 11, 12) sts, work to end of row.

Work 1 row even.

Dec 1 st armhole edge [every row] 3 (5, 5, 5, 7, 9, 9) times, then [every RS row] 3 (4, 4, 5, 4, 5, 7) times.

Cont neck shaping and work armhole edge even until armhole measures 7¾ (7¾, 8¼, 8¾, 9, 9¼, 9¾)", ending with a WS row—8 (9, 10, 13, 13, 16, 17) sts.

Shoulder shaping
Next row (RS) BO 4 (4, 6, 6, 6, 8, 8) sts, work to end.

Work 1 row even.

BO rem 4 (5, 6, 7, 7, 8, 9) sts.

RIGHT FRONT
With smaller needles, CO 38 (46, 50, 54, 62, 66, 74) sts.

Work in rib as for Back, ending with a RS row.

Change to larger needles.

Dec row (WS): P10 (6, 5, 4, 6, 11, 4) [p2tog, k12 (6, 7, 8, 6, 9, 8)] 2 (5, 5, 5, 7, 5, 7) times—36 (41, 45, 49, 55, 61, 67) sts.

Waist shaping
Beg Diamond patt and work 2 row even.

Dec row (RS): Work to last 3 sts, k2tog, k1.

Rep Dec row [every 6 (8, 8, 8, 10, 6, 8) rows] 5 (4, 4, 3, 1, 6, 1) time(s) more, then [every 0 (0, 0, 10, 12, 0, 10) rows] 0 (0, 0, 1, 2, 0, 3) times—30 (36, 40, 44, 51, 54, 62) sts.

Work 7 rows even.

Inc row (RS): Work to last st, M1, k1.

Rep Inc row [every 10 (10, 10, 10, 10, 8, 10) rows] 4 (3, 3, 2, 1, 2, 2) times more, then [every 0 (12, 12, 12, 12, 10, 12) rows] 0 (1, 1, 2, 3, 3, 3) times.

Work side edge even until piece measures 13¼ (13¾, 13¾, 14¼, 14½, 14¾, 14¾)", ending with a RS row, then go to Armhole shaping.

Neck shaping
At the same time, when piece measures 9¾ (10, 10¼, 11, 11¼, 11½, 11¾)", ending with a RS row, start neck shaping as follows: Ssk, work to end of row.

Rep dec at neck edge every 6 (4, 6, 4, 4, 4, 4) rows 9 (1, 15, 5, 13, 6, 14) times more, then every 8 (6, 0, 6, 6, 6, 6) rows 4 (14, 0, 12, 7, 12, 7) times.

Armhole shaping

Next row (WS): BO 7 (7, 8, 8, 11, 11, 12) sts, work to end.

Dec 1 st armhole edge [every row] 3 (5, 5, 5, 7, 9, 9) times, then [every RS row] 3 (4, 4, 5, 4, 5, 7) times.

Cont neck shaping and work armhole edge even until armhole measures 7¾ (7¾, 8¼, 8¾, 9, 9¼, 9¾)", ending with a RS row—8 (9, 10, 13, 13, 16, 17) sts.

Shoulder shaping

Next row (WS): BO (4, 6, 6, 6, 8, 8) sts, work to end.

Work 1 row even.

BO rem 4 (5, 6, 7, 7, 8, 9) sts.

Finishing

Weave in all ends. Block to finished measurements. Sew shoulder seams. Sew side seams.

Front band

With RS facing and longer circular needle, beg at lower right front edge, pick up and knit 59 (59, 61, 66, 68, 70, 70) sts to beg of neck shaping, 71 (73, 74, 76, 79, 81, 82) sts to right shoulder seam, 38 (38, 40, 42, 44, 44, 46) sts across back to left shoulder seam, 71 (73, 74, 76, 79, 81, 82) sts from left shoulder seam to beg of neck shaping, and 59 (59, 61, 66, 68, 70, 70) sts to end—298 (302, 310, 326, 338, 346, 350) sts.

Work 5 rows in K2, P2 Rib.

Buttonhole row (RS): Work 4 (4, 3, 3, 4, 3, 3) sts in rib, work [1-row 4-st] buttonhole, *work 7 (7, 8, 9, 9, 7, 7) sts in rib, work [1-row 4-st] buttonhole; rep from * 3 (3, 3, 3, 3, 4, 4) times more, work to end of row.

Work 4 rows in est rib.

BO all sts loosely in rib.

Armhole band

With RS facing and shorter circular needle, beg at shoulder seam, pick up and knit 48 (48, 52, 56, 58, 60, 64) sts to underarm seam and 48 (48, 52, 56, 58, 60, 64) sts from underarm seam to shoulder seam; place marker for beg of rnd and join—96 (96, 104, 112, 116, 120, 128) sts.

Work 6 rnds in K2, P2 Rib.

BO all sts loosely in rib.

Weave in all rem ends.

Cut a length of grosgrain ribbon 1" (2.5cm) longer than the left front edge (from bottom to shoulder seam). With needle and thread, sew onto middle of ribbed band, turning under ½" (1.25cm) at top and bottom.

Bow: Cut length of ribbon approx 25" (63.5cm) long. Fold bow following diagram. Tack onto left front neck.

Place markers on left front rib matching buttonhole positions. Sew on buttons.

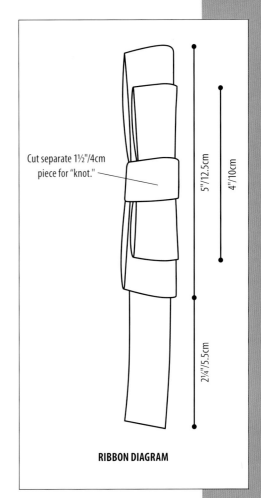

Cut separate 1½"/4cm piece for "knot."

5"/12.5cm

4"/10cm

2¼"/5.5cm

RIBBON DIAGRAM

Elegant Fitted Pullover

Design by Michele Rose Orne

I've always loved visiting vintage clothing shops as well as looking at old knitting patterns for inspiration. Usually the sizing has to change a bit, but so many of the styles of the 1930s, 1940s, and 1950s still hold great appeal. This vintage design came from a search of old pattern photos on the Internet. I didn't have the pattern, but just took inspiration from the photo for this sporty yet feminine design.

Sizes

Woman's small (medium, large, extra-large, 2X-large)

Instructions are given for smallest size, with larger sizes in parentheses. When only 1 number is given, it applies to all sizes.

Finished Measurements

Bust: 32 (36, 40, 44, 48)"/81.5 (91.5, 101.5, 112, 122)cm

Length to shoulders: 22 (22, 22½, 23¾, 24¼)"/56 (56, 57, 60.5, 61.5)cm

Materials

• Classic Elite *Wool Bam Boo* (DK weight; 50% wool/50% bamboo; 118 yd/108m per 1¾ oz/50g ball): 14 (15, 17, 18, 20) balls Vanilla #1650

• Size 3 (3.25mm) 16" (40cm) circular needle

• Size 4 (3.5mm) straight needles or size needed to obtain gauge

• Size E/4 (3.5mm) crochet hook

• Stitch holders

• Tapestry needle

Gauge

32 sts and 34 rows = 4" (10cm) in Broken Rib with larger needles.

Adjust needle size as necessary to obtain correct gauge.

Pattern Notes

- This garment is knit with an allover rib-type stitch, so it has a lot of stretch. Measurements taken on the flat may seem small, but the garment will stretch when worn.

- Front armhole measurement is ½" (1.25cm) longer than back armhole measurement. This means that the shoulder seam lays ½" (1.25cm) more to the back of the garment rather than centered at top of shoulder.

- When sewing the sleeves into the armhole, pin center of sleeve ½" (1.25cm) toward front of shoulder seam. This will make the center of the sleeve-pleat line up with the top of the shoulders.

- Read the pattern through completely before beginning because many shaping and patterning details occur simultaneously.

Stitch Pattern

BROKEN RIB (multiple of 2 sts + 1)
Rows 1 (RS) – 3: Work rib as already established.

Row 4 (WS): Knit.

Rep Rows 1–4 for pat.

CENTER FRONT PANEL (5 sts to begin)
See Chart, which shows the first 10 rows; continue working cable turns at edges to increase St st center section until indicated in pattern, after which work all sts in St st.

Instructions

BACK
With larger needles, CO 121 (137, 153, 169, 185) sts.

Set-up rib (WS): P1, *k1, p1; rep from * to end.

Next row (RS): K1, *p1, k1; rep from * to end.

Cont in est rib until piece measures 2¾" (7cm), ending with a RS row.

Next row (WS): Knit.

Begin working Broken Rib pat, lining up knit and purl sts with est rib below and work 4 rows even.

Inc row (RS): K1, M1, work in est pat to last st, M1, k1—123 (139, 155, 171, 187) sts.

Working new sts into pat, work 7 (7, 7, 9, 9) rows even, then rep Inc row—125 (141, 157, 173, 189) sts.

Work 11 (11, 11, 13, 13) rows even, then rep Inc row—127 (143, 159, 175, 191) sts.

Work even until piece measures 14¾ (14¾, 14¾, 15½, 15½)", ending with a WS row.

Shape armholes
Next 2 rows: BO 4 (6, 8, 8, 10) sts at armhole edge, work to end—119 (131, 143, 159, 171) sts.

Next 2 rows: BO 1 (2, 4, 6, 8) sts at armhole edge, work to end—117 (125, 135, 147, 155) sts.

BO 0 (1, 2, 2, 2) st(s) at beg of next 4 rows—117 (121, 127, 139, 147) sts.

BO 0 (0, 1, 1, 1) st(s) at beg of next 0 (0, 2, 10, 14) rows—117 (121, 125, 129, 133) sts.

Work even until armhole measures 7 (7, 7½, 8, 8½)", ending with a WS row.

Shape back neck and shoulders
Mark center 25 (25, 27, 27, 29) sts.

Row 1 (RS): BO 8 (9, 9, 9, 10), sts, work in pat to marked sts, join a 2nd ball of yarn, work across center 25 (25, 27, 27, 29) sts and put on holder for back neck, work to end.

Working both sides at once with separate balls of yarn, continue as follows:

Row 2: BO 8 (9, 9, 9, 10) sts, work to back neck; BO 8 sts, work to end.

Row 3: BO 8 (8, 9, 9, 9) sts, work to back neck; BO 8 sts, work to end.

Row 4: BO 8 (8, 9, 9, 9) sts, work to back neck; BO 5 sts, work to end.

Row 5: BO 8 (8, 8, 9, 9) sts, work to back neck; BO 5 sts, work to end.

Row 6: BO 8 (8, 8, 9, 9) sts, work to back neck; BO 2 sts, work to end.

Row 7: BO 7 (8, 8, 9, 9) sts, work to back neck; BO 2 sts, work to end.

Row 8: BO 7 (8, 8, 9, 9) sts.

FRONT
With larger needles, CO 121 (137, 153, 169, 185) sts.

Set-up rib (WS): K1, *p1, k1; rep from * to end.

Next row (RS): P1, *k1, p1; rep from * to end.

Cont in est rib until piece measures 2¾" (7cm), ending with a RS row.

Next row (WS): Knit.

Begin working Broken Rib pat, lining up knit and purl sts with est rib below.

Cont as for back until piece measures approx 12 (12, 12, 12¾, 12¾)"/30.5 (30.5, 30.5, 32.5, 32.5)cm, ending with Row 4 of Broken Rib pat—127 (143, 159, 175, 191) sts.

Next row (RS): Work 61 (69, 77, 85, 93) sts in est pat; work Center Front Panel over next 5 sts (see chart); work in est pat to end of row.

Cont working Broken Rib pat at sides and Center Front Panel as charted over center sts; after 10 rows of chart are complete, cont to increase the panel by 2 sts every RS row as established until there are 27 (29, 30, 32, 33) sts in Broken Rib on either side of panel.

Shape armholes
At the same time, when piece measures same as back to armhole, work armhole shaping as for back.

Left front placket, neck, and shoulder
Also, at the same time, when armhole measures 1 (1, 1½, 2, 2½)"/2.5 (2.5, 4, 5, 6.5)cm, ending with a WS row, work opening for center placket as follows:

Mark center st.

Row 1 (RS): Work in est pats through marked center st; slip rem sts to holder for right front.

Row 2: [P1-tbl, k1] twice; work in est pats to end of row.

Row 3: Work to last 4 sts, [p1, k1-tbl] twice.

Rep Rows 2 and 3 once.

Eyelet row (RS): Work to last 4 sts, yo, k2tog, p1, k1-tbl.

Cont to work est pats, complete armhole shaping (if necessary) and rep Eyelet row [every 8 rows] 4 times—59 (61, 63, 65, 67) sts rem when armhole shaping is complete.

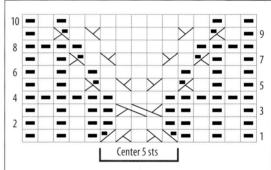

CENTER FRONT PANEL

Center 5 sts

Note: This is set-up of panel; continue as established

STITCH KEY

☐ K on RS, p on WS

■ P on RS, k on WS

Sl 1 to cn and hold in back; k1; p1 from cn

Sl 1 to cn and hold in front; p1; k1 from cn

Sl 1 to cn and hold in front; k2; k1 from cn

Sl 1 to cn and hold in back; p1, k1; k1 from cn

Sl 2 to cn and hold in front; k1; k1, p1 from cn

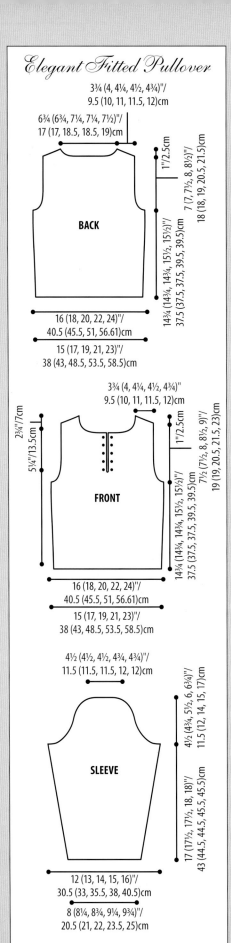

Elegant Fitted Pullover

BACK

3¾ (4, 4¼, 4½, 4¾)"/
9.5 (10, 11, 11.5, 12)cm

6¾ (6¾, 7¼, 7¼, 7½)"/
17 (17, 18.5, 18.5, 19)cm

1"/2.5cm

7 (7, 7½, 8, 8½)"/
18 (18, 19, 20.5, 21.5)cm

14¾ (14¾, 14¾, 15½, 15½)"/
37.5 (37.5, 37.5, 39.5, 39.5)cm

16 (18, 20, 22, 24)"/
40.5 (45.5, 51, 56.61)cm

15 (17, 19, 21, 23)"/
38 (43, 48.5, 53.5, 58.5)cm

FRONT

3¾ (4, 4¼, 4½, 4¾)"
9.5 (10, 11, 11.5, 12)cm

2¾"/7cm

5¼"/13.5cm

1"/2.5cm

7½ (7½, 8, 8½, 9)"/
19 (19, 20.5, 21.5, 23)cm

14¾ (14¾, 14¾, 15½, 15½)"/
37.5 (37.5, 37.5, 39.5, 39.5)cm

16 (18, 20, 22, 24)"/
40.5 (45.5, 51, 56.61)cm

15 (17, 19, 21, 23)"/
38 (43, 48.5, 53.5, 58.5)cm

SLEEVE

4½ (4½, 4½, 4¾, 4¾)"/
11.5 (11.5, 11.5, 12, 12)cm

4½ (4¾, 5½, 6, 6¾)"/
11.5 (12, 14, 15, 17)cm

17 (17½, 17½, 18, 18)"/
43 (44.5, 44.5, 45.5, 45.5)cm

12 (13, 14, 15, 16)"/
30.5 (33, 35.5, 38, 40.5)cm

8 (8¼, 8¾, 9¼, 9¾)"/
20.5 (21, 22, 23.5, 25)cm

At the same time, when there are 32 (32, 33, 33, 34) sts in center section and 27 (29, 30, 32, 33) sts in Rib section, stop increasing center section, working panel even in St st to shoulder.

When placket measures 5¼" (13.5cm), ending with a RS row, shape neck as follows:

Next row (WS): BO 13 (13, 14, 14, 15) sts, work in pat to end—46 (48, 49, 51, 52) sts.

Cont binding off at beg of next 6 WS rows (neck edge): [5 sts] once, [4 sts] once, [3 sts] once, [1 st] 3 times—31 (33, 34, 36, 37) sts rem.

Work even until armhole measures 7½ (7½, 8, 8½, 9)", ending with a WS row.

At beg of next 4 RS rows, BO 8 (9, 9, 9, 10) sts once, 8 (8, 9, 9, 9) sts once, 8 (8, 8, 9, 9) sts once, and 7 (8, 8, 9, 9) sts once.

Right front placket, neck, and shoulder
Slip right front sts back to left needle with RS facing and rejoin yarn.

Row 1 (RS): M1 in center st, work in est pats to end of row—1 st inc'd.

Row 2: Work in est pats to last 4 sts, [k1, p1-tbl] twice.

Row 3: [K1-tbl, p1] twice, work in est pats to end of row.

Rep Rows 2 and 3 once more.

Eyelet row (RS): K1-tbl, p1, ssk, yo, work to end of row.

Cont to work est pats, complete armhole shaping (if necessary) and rep Eyelet row [every 8 rows] 4 times—59 (61, 63, 65, 67) sts rem when armhole shaping is complete.

At the same time, when there are 32 (32, 33, 33, 34) sts in center section and 27 (29, 30, 32, 33) sts in Rib section, stop increasing center section, working panel even in St st to shoulder.

When placket measures 5¼" (13.5cm), ending with a WS row, shape neck as follows:

Next row (RS): BO 13 (13, 14, 14, 15) sts, work pat to end—46 (48, 49, 51, 52) sts.

Cont binding off at beg of next 6 RS rows (neck edge): [5 sts] once, [4 sts] once, [3 sts] once, [1 st] 3 times—31 (33, 34, 36, 37) sts rem.

Work even until armhole measures 7½ (7½, 8, 8½, 9)", ending with a RS row.

At beg of next 4 WS rows, BO 8 (9, 9, 9, 10) sts once, 8 (8, 9, 9, 9) sts once, 8 (8, 8, 9, 9) sts once, and 7 (8, 8, 9, 9) sts once.

SLEEVES
With larger needles, CO 63 (65, 69, 73, 77) sts.

Set-up rib (WS): P1, *k1, p1; rep from * to end.

Next row (RS): K1, *p1, k1; rep from * to end.

Work in est rib until cuff measures 3" (7.5cm), ending with a RS row.

Next row (WS): Knit across.

Inc row (RS): K1, M1, work Broken Rib to last st (lining up knit and purl sts with rib below), M1, k1—65 (67, 71, 75, 79) sts.

Rep Inc row [every 4 rows] 0 (2, 8, 12 18) times, every 6 rows 11 (17, 13, 11, 7) times, and every 8 rows 5 (0, 0, 0, 0) times, working new sts into pat as they accumulate—97 (105, 113, 121, 129) sts.

Work even until piece measures 17 (17½, 17½, 18, 18)" or desired length to armhole, ending with a WS row.

Shape sleeve cap

Rows 1 and 2: BO 4 (6, 8, 8, 10) sts, work to end—89 (93, 97, 105, 109) sts.

Rows 3 and 4: BO 2 (3, 3, 3, 3) sts, work to end—85 (87, 91, 99, 103) sts.

Rows 5 and 6: BO 2 sts, work to end—81 (83, 87, 95, 99) sts.

Dec 1 st each end [every RS row] 2 (2, 3, 3, 3) times—77 (79, 81, 89, 93) sts.

Dec 1 st each end [every 4th row] 1 (1, 1, 2, 3) times—75 (77, 79, 85, 87) sts.

Dec 1 st each end [every 6th row] 1 (1, 2, 2, 2) times—73 (75, 75, 81, 83) sts.

Dec 1 st each end [every RS row] 3 (4, 4, 5, 5) times, ending with a WS row—67 (67, 67, 73, 73) sts.

Next 6 (6, 6, 8, 8) rows: BO 2 sts, work to end of row—55 (55, 55, 57, 57) sts.

Next 4 rows: BO 3 sts, work to end of row—43 (43, 43, 45, 45) sts.

Next 2 rows: BO 4 sts, work to end of row—35 (35, 35, 37, 37) sts.

BO rem sts.

Finishing

Weave in all ends. Block pieces to finished measurements, being careful not to crush ribbed sections.

Sew shoulder seams.

Neck trim

With RS facing, using circular needle and beg at right front placket edge, pick up and knit 38 (38, 39, 39, 40) sts along right front neck edge, then 14 sts along right back neck edge; knit 25 (25, 27, 27, 29) sts from center back st holder; pick up and knit 14 sts along left back neck edge, then 38 (38, 39, 39, 40) sts along left front neck edge—129 (129, 133, 133, 137) sts.

Row 1 (WS): [P1-tbl, k1] twice, purl to last 4 sts, [k1, p1-tbl] twice.

Row 2 (RS): [K1-tbl, p1] twice; k1, *p1, k1; rep from * to last 4 sts; [p1, k1-tlb] twice.

Row 3: Rep Row 1.

BO.

Make dart in sleeve caps

Fold sleeve cap so that approx 1" (2.5cm) at center is on top with ½" (1.25cm) folding beneath back toward center, then another ½" (1.25cm) beneath that folding back out to sides. Baste pleat in place to hold. Sew cap into armhole, making sure to align center of sleeve darts ½" (1.25cm) forward of shoulder seam. (Shoulder seams should be ½" (1.25cm) toward back of shoulder.) Sew side and sleeve seams.

Neck lacing cord

With crochet hook, work chain st for approx 15" (38cm).

Thread cord through lacing holes at center front placket.

Smart Woven Jacket

Design by Anna Bell

I wanted a between-seasons jacket (or for wearing indoors during winter) that would be a super-quick knit. The basketweave pattern makes a stretchy fabric that gently hugs the figure, giving the jacket its fit. An integral slip-stitch edge at the front opening gives structure and reinforces the buttonholes.

Size

To fit bust size 32–34, (36–38, 40–42, 42–44, 44–48)"/81–86 (91–97, 102–107, 107–112, 112–122)cm

Instructions are given for smallest size, with larger sizes in parentheses. When only 1 number is given, it applies to all sizes.

Finished Measurements

Chest: 34¾ (37¼, 40, 42¾, 45¼)"/88.5 (94.5, 101.5, 108.5, 115)cm

Length to shoulder: 21½ (22½, 23, 23½, 24½)"/54.5 (57, 58.5, 59.5, 62) cm

Materials 3

• Rowan *Pure Wool DK* (DK weight; 100% superwash merino wool; 137 yd/127m per 1¾ oz/50g ball): 12 (13, 14, 15, 16) balls Scarlet #041

• Size 11 (8mm) needles or size needed to obtain gauge

• Spare needle, same size or smaller than main needle

• Large crochet hook (for cast-on)

• Size F/5 (3.75mm) crochet hook (for button covers)

• Seven 1" (2.5cm) plastic shank buttons

• Tapestry needle

Gauge

12 sts and 16 rows = 4" (10cm) in Basketweave pat with 2 strands yarn held tog.

Adjust needle size as necessary to obtain correct gauge.

Pattern Notes

- Two strands of yarn are held together throughout.
- Selvedge stitches are worked in stockinette stitch.

Special Abbreviation

P1f&b: Purl in front and back of st.

Special Techniques

Provisional cast-on: With crochet hook and waste yarn, make a chain several sts longer than desired cast-on. With knitting needle and project yarn, pick up indicated number of sts in the "bumps" on back of chain. When indicated in pattern, "unzip" the crochet chain to free live sts.

1-row, 2-st buttonhole: With RS facing, work to desired position for buttonhole. Bring yarn to front and sl 1 pwise, bring yarn to back of work; *sl 1 pwise, pass the 2nd slipped st over the first as if to BO; rep from * once (2 sts bound off); slip last st on RH needle back to LH needle. Turn work. Using cable method, CO 3 sts on LH needle; turn work. Slip first st on LH needle pwise, then pass the last cast-on st over this st. Continue knitting.

Stitch Patterns

BASKETWEAVE PATTERN
(multiple of 4 sts)
Row 1 (RS): Knit.

Row 2 and all WS rows: Work the sts as they present themselves, i.e. purl the purl sts and knit the knit sts.

Row 3: *P2, k2; rep from * across.

Row 5: Knit.

Row 7: *K2, p2; rep from * across.

Row 8: Rep Row 2.

Rep Rows 1–8 for pat.

SEED STITCH
Row 1 (RS): *K1, p1; rep from * to end.

Row 2: Knit the purl sts and purl the knit sts as they face you.

Rep Row 2 for pat.

DOUBLE-KNIT FRONT EDGE (4 sts)
At each front edge (RS and WS): [sl 1 wyif, k1] twice.

Instructions

BACK
Hem
With yarn held double and using provisional method, CO 54 (58, 62, 66, 70) sts.

Beg with a WS row, work 3 rows St st.

Turning row (RS): Purl.

Next row: Purl.

Pat set-up row: K1 (selvedge st), *k2, p2; rep from * to last st, k1 (selvedge st).

Next row: P1,*p2, k2; rep from * to last st, p1.

Hem joining row (RS): Unzip provisional cast-on and put live sts on spare needle. Fold work on Turning row with RS facing. With needles parallel and cast-on sts in back, *k1 from front needle tog with 1 from back needle; rep from * to end to join hem.

Body
Purl 1 row.

Beg with Row 3 and maintaining selvedge sts in St st, work even in Basketweave pat until piece measures approx 14 (14½, 15, 15, 15½)" from Turning row, ending with a WS row.

Shape armholes

BO 2 (2, 3, 3, 4) sts at beg of next 2 rows—50 (54, 56, 60, 62) sts.

Dec row (RS): K1, k2tog, work in pat to last 3 sts, ssk, k1—48 (52, 54, 58, 60) sts.

Rep Dec row [every other row] 3 (4, 4, 5, 5) times—42 (44, 46, 48, 50) sts.

Work even until armholes measure 6 (6½, 6½, 7, 7½)", ending with a WS row.

Shape back neck and shoulders

Next row (RS): Work 14 (14, 15, 16, 16) sts; join 2nd ball of yarn and BO center 14 (16, 16, 16, 18) sts; work 14 (14, 15, 16, 16) sts to end of row.

Next 4 rows: Working both sides at once with separate balls of yarn, BO 2 sts at each neck edge twice—10 (10, 11, 12, 12) sts each side.

Work 1 row even.

Dec row (RS): Work to 2 sts from neck edge, k2tog; ssk, work to end—9 (9, 10, 11, 11) sts each side.

Work even until armholes measure 7½ (8, 8, 8½, 9)", ending with a WS row.

Next 2 rows: BO 4 (4, 5, 5, 5) sts at beg of each row—5 (5, 5, 6, 6) sts rem each side.

Next 2 rows: BO off rem sts at beg of each row.

LEFT FRONT

Hem

With yarn held double and using provisional method, CO 28 (30, 32, 34, 36) sts.

Beg with a WS row, work 3 rows St st.

Turning row (RS): Purl.

Next row: Purl.

Pat set-up row: K1 (selvedge st), *k2, p2; rep from * to last st, k1 (selvedge st).

Next row: P1, *k2, p2; rep from * to last st, p1.

Hem joining row (RS): Unzip provisional cast-on and put live sts on spare needle. Fold work on Turning row with RS facing. Knit each st together with its equivalent on cast-on edge to join hem.

Inc row (WS): P1f&b twice, work est Basketweave pat to last st, p1—30 (32, 34, 36, 38) sts.

Next row: K1, work in est Basketweave pat to last 4 sts, [sl 1 wyif, k1] twice.

Work even in Basketweave pat, maintaining side seam selvedge st in St st and 4-st double-knitting at front edge, until piece measures 14 (14½, 15, 15, 15½)", ending with a WS row.

Shape armhole

Next row (RS): BO 2 (2, 3, 3, 4) sts, work in pat to end of row—28 (30, 31, 33, 34) sts.

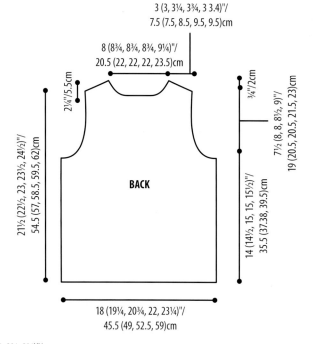

Smart Woven Jacket

BACK

3 (3, 3¼, 3¾, 3 3.4)"/
7.5 (7.5, 8.5, 9.5, 9.5)cm

8 (8¾, 8¾, 8¾, 9¼)"/
20.5 (22, 22, 22, 23.5)cm

2¼"/5.5cm

¾"/2cm

7½ (8, 8, 8½, 9)"/
19 (20.5, 20.5, 21.5, 23)cm

21½ (22½, 23, 23½, 24½)"/
54.5 (57, 58.5, 59.5, 62)cm

14 (14½, 15, 15½)"/
35.5 (37.38, 39.5)cm

18 (19¼, 20¾, 22, 23¼)"/
45.5 (49, 52.5, 59)cm

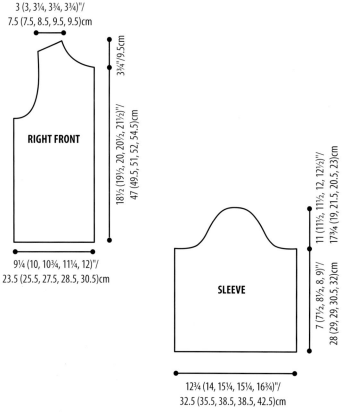

RIGHT FRONT

3 (3, 3¼, 3¾, 3¾)"/
7.5 (7.5, 8.5, 9.5, 9.5)cm

3¾"/9.5cm

18½ (19½, 20, 20½, 21½)"/
47 (49.5, 51, 52, 54.5)cm

9¼ (10, 10¾, 11¼, 12)"/
23.5 (25.5, 27.5, 28.5, 30.5)cm

SLEEVE

11 (11½, 11½, 12, 12½)"/
17¾ (19, 21.5, 20.5, 23)cm

7 (7½, 8½, 8, 9)"/
28 (29, 29, 30.5, 32)cm

12¾ (14, 15¼, 15¼, 16¾)"/
32.5 (35.5, 38.5, 38.5, 42.5)cm

Work 1 row even.

Dec row (RS): K1, k2tog, work in pat to end—27 (29, 30, 32, 33) sts.

Rep Dec row [every RS row] 3 (4, 4, 5, 5) times—24 (25, 26, 27, 28) sts.

Work even until armhole measures 4½ (5, 5, 5½, 6)", ending with a RS row.

Shape neck and shoulder
Next row (WS): BO 10 (11, 11, 11, 12) sts, work in pat to end of row—14 (14, 15, 16, 16) sts.

Work 1 row even.

Dec row (WS): P2tog, work in pat to end of row—13 (13, 14, 15, 15) sts.

Rep Dec row [every WS row] 4 times—9 (9, 10, 11, 11) sts.

Work even until armhole measures 7½ (8, 8, 8½, 9)", ending with a WS row.

Next row (RS): BO 4 (4, 5, 5, 5) sts, work in pat to end—5 (5, 5, 5, 6) sts.

Work 1 row even.

BO rem sts.

Place markers for 7 buttons evenly along front opening edge and use them as reference for placement of buttonholes on right front.

RIGHT FRONT
With yarn held double and using provisional method, CO 28 (30, 32, 34, 36) sts.

Beg with a WS row, work 3 rows St st.

Turning row (RS): Purl.

Next row: Purl.

Pat set-up row (RS): K1, p2 (0, 2, 0, 2), *k2, p2; rep from * to last st, k1.

Next row: P1, *k2, p2; rep from * to last 3 (1, 3, 1, 3) sts, k2 (0, 3, 0, 2), p1.

Hem joining row (RS): Unzip provisional cast-on and put live sts on spare needle. Fold work on Turning row with RS facing. Knit each st together with its equivalent on cast-on edge to join hem.

Inc row (WS): Purl to last 2 sts, p1f&b twice—30 (32, 34, 36, 38) sts.

Next row: [Sl 1 wyif, k1] twice, work in est Basketweave pat to last st, k1.

Work even in Basketweave pat, maintaining single edge st in St st at seam edge and 4-st double-knitting at front edge and *at the same time* work a 1-row buttonhole (or use your preferred method) on RS rows that correspond to stitch markers on left front as follows:

Buttonhole row (RS): Work 4 edging sts, work 1 st in pat, work buttonhole, cont in est pat to end.

Work even until piece measures 14 (14½, 15, 15, 15½)", ending with a RS row.

Shape armholes
Next row (WS): BO 2 (2, 3, 3, 4) sts, work in est pat to end of row—28 (30, 31, 33, 34) sts.

Dec row (RS): Work in pat to last 3 sts, ssk, k1—27 (29, 30, 32, 33) sts.

Rep Dec row [every RS row] 3 (4, 4, 5, 5) times—24 (25, 26, 27, 28) sts.

Work even until armhole measures 4½ (5, 5, 5½, 6)"/11.5 (12.5, 12.5, 14, 15)cm, ending with a WS row.

Shape neck and shoulder
Next row (RS): BO 10 (11, 11, 11, 12), work in pat to end—14 (14, 15, 16, 16) sts. Work 1 row even.

Dec row (RS): Ssk, work in pat to end—13 (13, 14, 15, 15) sts.

Rep Dec row [every RS row] 4 times—9 (9, 10, 11, 11) sts.

Work even until armhole measures 7½ (8, 8, 8½, 9)", ending with a RS row.

Next row (WS): BO 4 (4, 5, 5, 5) sts, work in pat to end—5 (5, 5, 5, 6) sts.

Work 1 row even.

BO rem sts.

SLEEVES
Hem
With yarn held double, CO 38 (42, 46, 46, 50) sts.

Beg with a WS row, work 3 rows St st.

Turning row (RS): Purl.

Next row: Purl.

Pat set-up row (RS): K3, *p2, k2; rep from * to last 3 sts, p2, k1.

Next row: P1, *k2, p2; rep from * to last st, p1.

Hem joining row (RS): Unzip provisional cast-on and put live sts on spare needle. Fold work on Turning row with RS facing. Knit each st together with its equivalent on cast-on edge to join hem.

Purl 1 row.

Beg with Row 3 of est Basketweave pat and maintaining edge sts in St st, work even until piece measures approx 11 (11½, 11½, 12, 12½)" from Turning row, ending with a WS row.

STITCH KEY

☐ K on RS, p on WS

▬ P on RS, k on WS

4-st rep

BASKETWEAVE

Shape sleeve cap

Next 2 rows: BO 3 sts, work in pat to end of row—32 (36, 40, 40, 44) sts.

Dec row (RS): K1, k2tog, work in pat to last 3 sts, ssk, k1—30 (34, 38, 38, 42) sts.

Rep Dec row [every RS row] 4 (5, 7, 7, 8) times—22 (24, 24, 24, 26) sts.

Work 3 rows even.

Rep Dec row on next row, then [every other RS row] 2 (2, 2, 1, 2) time(s)—18 (20, 20, 22, 22) sts.

Next 4 rows: BO 3 sts, work in pat to end—6 (8, 8, 10, 10) sts.

BO rem sts.

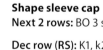

Finishing

Weave in ends.

Block all pieces to finished measurements.

Sew shoulder seams.

Collar

With RS facing, yarn held double, and beg and ending 1½" (3.75cm) from front edges, pick up and knit 58 (62, 66, 70, 74) sts evenly around neck.

Set-up row (WS): P1f&b twice; *k1, p1; rep from * to last 2 sts, p1f&b twice—62 (66, 70, 74, 78) sts.

Row 1: [Sl 1 wyif, k1] twice, k1f&b into next st, work in est seed st to last 4 sts, [sl 1 wyif, k1] twice.

Rep Row 1 until collar measures 3" (7.5cm).

Knit 3 rows.

BO very loosely.

Set in sleeves. Sew side and sleeve seams.

Crochet button covers

With single strand of main yarn and crochet hook, ch 2.

Rnd 1: Work 8 sc into 2nd ch from hook.

Rnd 2: Work 2 sc into each sc around—16 sc.

Check to see whether this will cover your button. If not, work 1 more rnd even.

Next rnd: Work 2 sc tog all around—8 sc.

Fasten off, leaving a 6" (15cm) tail.

Cover the button, then with tail and tapestry needle, close the bottom of the cover around button shank by going in and out of opposite loops until secure.

Sew buttons to left front opposite buttonholes.

Very 1940s Snood

Design by Elanor Lynn

Some twenty years ago, at college, I had a vintage blue snood. I used to wear it with my "Andrews Sisters" suits or wooly sweaters and skirts during wintery Vermont autumns. Lost, or jettisoned long ago during one of my dozens of moves, it's been recreated here in Shetland Cane Stitch pattern. You could embellish the headband with any number of flowers or frills, as was typical of snoods from the 1940s, or leave it plain as shown here for a sleeker look. With practice, you'll master arranging your hair inside the snood to create fullness at the bottom. For the classic 1940s profile, style the front section of your hair into a high pouf with a couple of bobby pins before securing the snood in place with bobby pins placed through the holes in the netting just behind the headband.

Size

One size

Finished Measurements

Width: Approx 12" (30.5cm), not including headband

Length: Approx 12" (30.5cm)

Materials

- Cascade *Heritage* (75% wool/25% nylon; 437 yd/400m per 3½ oz/100g skein): 1 skein blue #3608
- Size 2 (2.75mm) 24" (60cm) circular needle or size needed to obtain gauge
- Size 5 (3.75mm) 24" (60cm) circular needle (optional for pat Row 3)
- Split-ring stitch markers (2 colors)
- Point protectors
- Tapestry needle
- Small crochet hook
- Black elastic cord
- Sewing needle and thread

Gauge

29 sts and 58 rows = 4" (10cm) in garter st on smaller needles.

Adjust needle size as necessary to obtain correct gauge.

Special Technique

Short rows: The snood is shaped by working short rows, turning the work in the middle of the row. Similar to turning a sock heel, you will work 1 more st from the sts on hold at the end of each row until all 73 sts are worked each row. *Note: Do not wrap end st when turning, as with other short rows.*

Pattern Notes

• Take time to really understand the stitch pattern before commencing work. Work 2 practice swatches: the first on larger needles and light-colored worsted weight yarn, then the second on the working needles and your project yarn.

• Since both garter stitch and the 3-row Cane stitch look the same on both sides, this snood is reversible. The terms "right side" and "wrong side" are used for convenience.

• Because of this reversibility, the chart is a bit unconventional. Each stitch symbol is shown *as it is worked*, whether on a RS or WS row. As usual, read the chart from right to left for "RS" rows and from left to right for "WS" rows as indicated by the position of the row numbers at the beginning of each row.

• The chart shows the first 19 rows of the pattern and short-row shaping. After completing the chart, continue in the same manner.

• When placing markers on either side of the center patterned area, use one color for first marker to mark the beginning of a "RS" row and another color for 2nd marker to mark the beginning of a "WS" row. This will help you keep track of which row you are working. Carefully note each row completed so that you won't get lost, because ripping back is tricky in this pattern.

• Row 3 should be knit loosely using a larger needle if necessary. This creates a more open fabric and facilitates the p3tog of Row 1. Or, if you knit "English" style, switch to continental style for Row 3.

• Use point protectors to prevent any possible dropped stitches.

• Beads can be knit into each p3tog.

• Each skein will yield two snoods.

Stitch Pattern

CANE STITCH (for practice swatch)
CO 19 sts.

Row 1: K2, *p3tog, yo twice; rep from * to last 2 sts, k2.

Row 2: K2, *work [k1, p1] into double-yo of previous row, k1; rep from * to last 2 sts, k2.

Row 3: Knit loosely, using larger needle if desired.

Rep Rows 1–3 for pat.

CANE STITCH (for snood)
Note: *When pat says to work to "last st," that means to "last st that's been brought into work on a previous row."* Slip markers as you come to them.

Row 1 (RS): K1, *p3tog, yo twice; rep from * to last st, k1, k1 st from those on hold.

Row 2 (WS): K2, *work [k1, p1] into double-yo of previous row, k1; rep from * to last st, k1; K1 st from those on hold.

Row 3 (RS): Knit loosely (using larger needle if desired) to end of working sts; knit 1 st from those on hold.

Row 4 (WS): K3, *p3tog, yo twice; rep from * to last 2 sts, k2; knit 1 st from those on hold.

Row 5 (RS): K3, *work [k1, p1] into double-yo of previous row, k1; rep from * to last 3 sts, k3; knit 1 st from those on hold; remove marker and place here.

Row 6 (WS): Knit loosely (using larger needle if desired) to end of working sts; knit 1 st from those on hold; remove marker and place here.

Rep Rows 1–6 for pat, moving markers 3 sts out on each side every 6 rows to incorporate 1 new pat rep each side when working the following 6 rows.

Instructions

HEADBAND
CO 189 sts.

Knit 2 rows.

Next 13 rows: K2tog, knit to last 2 sts, k2tog—163 sts.

Next row: K2tog, BO 44 sts (including the k2tog), knit to last 2 sts, k2tog—117 sts.

Next row: BO 44 sts, knit to end—73 sts.

SNOOD
Row 1 (RS): K22, pm, k1, *p3tog, [yo twice]; rep from * 8 times, k1, pm, k1, turn—29 sts between markers, 21 sts rem on LH needle.

Row 2: Work in est pat following chart or st pat instructions to marker, knit 1 st from those on hold.

Cont in Cane st, working 1 additional st at the end of each row. After every 6th row, move markers 3 sts toward selvedges in order to incorporate new sts into pat on following row. Cont until all 73 sts are incorporated.

Next row: K2, work in pat to last 2 sts, k2.

Maintaining first and last 2 sts in garter st, work even until piece measures approx 12½" (32cm) measured from center of garter band, ending with Row 3 or 6.

Dec row: K2, *p3tog, yo *(note: single, not a double yarnover)*; rep from * to last 2 sts, k2—50 sts.

Knit 2 rows.

Dec row: K2, *p2tog; rep from * to last 2 sts, k2—27 sts.

Knit 1 row.

Dec row: K2, *k2tog; rep from * to last 3 sts, k3—16 sts.

Knit 1 row.

Dec row: K2, *k2tog; rep from * to last 2 sts, k2—10 sts.

Knit 1 row.

Dec row: K2tog across—5 sts.

BO.

Finishing

Edging

With "RS" facing, beg at point where left headband meets the snood, pick up and knit 1 st from headband edge, pick up and knit 1 st in each st along snood to 5 bound-off sts, skip the bound-off sts, pick up and knit 1 st in each st to headband edge, pick up and knit 1 st from headband edge.

Bind off tightly.

Weave in all ends.

Block to finished measurements.

Using a crochet hook, thread elastic through edging and adjust to desired fit (about 12–13" (30.5–33cm) or longer if you have lots of hair). Secure elastic ends with sewing thread.

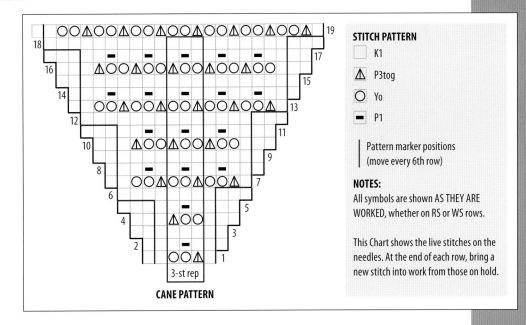

CANE PATTERN

STITCH PATTERN

☐	K1
△	P3tog
O	Yo
▬	P1

| Pattern marker positions (move every 6th row)

NOTES:
All symbols are shown AS THEY ARE WORKED, whether on RS or WS rows.

This Chart shows the live stitches on the needles. At the end of each row, bring a new stitch into work from those on hold.

Crocheted Circle Skirt

Design by Ellen Brys

In the spirit of the many vintage knitting pattern books that mixed in a few crochet patterns without missing a beat, we couldn't resist including this lovely crocheted skirt in this collection. (If crochet is not your thing, don't despair; instructions for knitting the skirt appear on page 94.) I designed this skirt with inspiration from my vast archive of vintage knitting and crocheting patterns from the 1930s and 1940s. My love of vintage clothing stems from my days of playing dress-up in my mother's clothes and landed me in fashion design school, where I scoured secondhand stores and flea markets for treasures and discovered knitting and crocheting patterns along the way. I especially loved the crocheted dresses and skirts, as they seemed so classy and feminine. I designed this skirt to have the flavor of the vintage skirts I admire and still be easy for someone to make.

Sizes

Woman's small (medium, large, extra-large)

Instructions are given for smallest size, with larger sizes in parentheses. When only 1 number is given, it applies to all sizes.

Finished Measurements

Length from top waistband: approx 22" (56cm)

Circumference at waist: 26¾ (30½, 34¼, 38)"/68 (77.5, 87, 96.5)cm

Circumference at hem: 40¼ (44, 47¾, 51½)"/ 102.5 (112, 121, 131)cm

Materials

- Halcyon Yarn *5/2 Pearl Cotton* (100% mercerized cotton; 2,000 yd/1,829m per 1 lb/450g cone; 300 yd/374m per 2.4 oz/68g mini-cone): 1 cone Natural #105 (A); 1 mini-cone Black #101 (B) *[Note: for extra-large, you might want to purchase 1 additional mini-cone A because, depending on your gauge, it may require a bit more than 1 lb.]*

- Size C/2 (2.75mm) crochet hook or size needed to obtain gauge

- Tapestry needle

Gauge

25 dc and 16 rnds = 4" (10cm).

Adjust hook size as necessary to obtain correct gauge.

- To change the size of this skirt, increase/ decrease the number of chains in increments of 12, bearing in mind that 12 dc = just under 2" (5cm).

- To increase the flare between waist and hem, work increase round more frequently (every 6 rnds or as desired).

- You will probably want to wear this skirt with a slip.

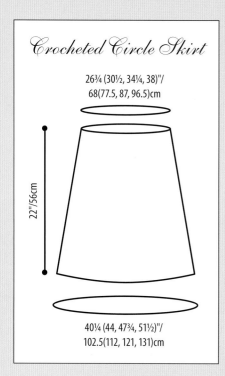

Crocheted Circle Skirt

26¾ (30½, 34¼, 38)"/
68(77.5, 87, 96.5)cm

22"/56cm

40¼ (44, 47¾, 51½)"/
102.5(112, 121, 131)cm

Stitch Pattern

SHELL
Work 5 dc in 1 st. On subsequent rnds, work the 5 dc in the 3rd dc of this group.

4 DC TOG CLUSTER
Work dc in each of next 4 sts, holding back last loop of each st, yo and draw through all 5 loops on hook.

Instructions

SKIRT BODY
With A, ch 216 (240, 264, 288) and join in a circle. Ch 3 and turn.

Rnd 1: *Make 4 dc in base of ch 3 (counts as first shell faggoting), skip 2 ch and dc in next 13 (15, 17, 19) sts (dc panel), skip 2 ch and make 5 dc in next st (shell faggoting), skip 2 ch, dc in next 15 sts; rep from * around, ending with sl st to top of ch 3 at beg of rnd to join. Turn. This makes a total of 12 panels of 13 (15, 17, 19) dc sts with shell faggoting between.

Rnd 2: Sl st into first dc, ch 3 and dc in next 12 (14, 16, 18) sts, *5-dc in 3rd st of 5-dc shell; 13 (15, 17, 19) dc in next dc sts; rep from * around, ending with sl st to top of ch 3 at beg to join. Ch 3 and turn.

Rnd 3: *Make 5-dc shell in top of shell and dc in each of 13 (15, 17, 19) dc; rep from * around, ending with sl st to top of ch 3 to join. Ch 3 and turn.

Rnd 4: Dc in 2nd dc and continue making dc in each dc and shell in top of each shell, ending with sl st in top of ch 3 at beg to join. Ch 3 and turn.

Rnd 5: Make shell in top of first shell and dc in each dc. Continue around, ending with sl st in top of ch 3 at beg to join. Ch 3 and turn.

Rnds 6–16: Rep [Rnds 4 and 5] 5 times, then work Rnd 4 once more.

Rnd 17 (Inc rnd): *Make shell in shell, 2 dc in first dc (increasing dc panel by 1 st), dc to next shell, work shell, dc in next 12 (14, 16, 18) dc, 2 dc in next dc; rep from * around to last st where you dc in base of first ch 3 (counts as 2 dc in one space for the inc), sl st to ch 3 at beg to join. Ch 3 and turn—14 (16, 18, 20) sts in each dc panel.

Rnds 18–26: Make shell in every shell st and dc in every dc. Ch 3 and turn.

Rep [Rnds 17–26] 5 times, then rep [Rnd 18] 3 times more—19 (21, 23, 25) sts in each dc panel.

Join as usual and fasten off. Weave in end of yarn.

WAISTBAND
Rnd 1: With A, make sc in top edge of skirt where you originally started (joining seam of skirt) and sc in each st along top of skirt, making 2 sc in each 2 ch space; join with sl st to first st of rnd. Ch 1 and turn.

Rnd 2: Sc in first st, *ch 2 and skip 2 sts, sc in next st; rep from * to end of rnd, finish with ch 2 and sl st to join to sc at beg of rnd. Ch 1 and turn.

Rnd 3: Sc in first st. Make 9 dc in 2nd ch 2 loop, *skip next ch 2 loop, sc in sc, skip next ch 2 loop, 9 dc in next ch 2 loop; rep from * , ending with 5 dc in last loop. Fasten off and weave in end. Turn skirt to continue waistband.

Note: The waistband st pat does not end in a perfect repeat, but the drawstring covers this, and it should not detract from the design.

Rnd 4: With B, attach to dc at end of last rnd, ch 2, *4 dc tog cluster, 1 dc , 4 dc tog cluster, ch 5, skip 1 st; rep from *, ending with 4 dc tog cluster, 1 dc, and join with sl st to first st of rnd. Ch 3 and turn.

Rnd 5: *Make sc in top of cluster, ch 5, sc in top of next cluster, ch 2; rep from *, ending with ch 2, sc in sc, ch 1, and turn.

Rnd 6: Sc in first sc, *9 dc in ch 2 loop, sc around both ch 5 loops from Rnds 4 and 5 and into skipped dc from Rnd 3 (ch 5 loops are secured with this st); rep from *, ending with 5 dc in last loop and join with sl st to sc at beg of rnd.

Fasten off and weave in end of yarn.

CIRCLE EDGING
First circle: With B, ch 5 and join with sl st to first ch to form a circle. Ch 3 (counts as first dc), make 18 dc in ring. Join with sl st to ch 3 and fasten off.

Next circles: Ch 5 and join as above, ch 3 and make 8 dc in ring, join with sl st to joining st of previous circle, make 9 more dc in ring to complete this circle. Join with sl st to ch 3. Fasten off.

Continue making circles in this way, joining to previous one for a total of 40 (44, 48, 52) circles. Do not fasten off yet. Attach circle edging by pinning to bottom of skirt, making sure to space evenly. If necessary, unravel extra circles or make additional ones to fit hem.

With B, sew circles to the skirt with sts at the top of the circle. Weave in all ends.

DRAWSTRING
Chain 405 (450, 510, 570) sts. Make 1 dc in 3rd ch from hook and in each ch until last st. Make 1 hdc in last st and sl st into base ch to curve end of drawstring. Tie off and weave in ends. Lace drawstring through the center holes of the circles on the waistband, omitting the center circle so the ends are outside the skirt on each side of the center.

Block to finished measurements.

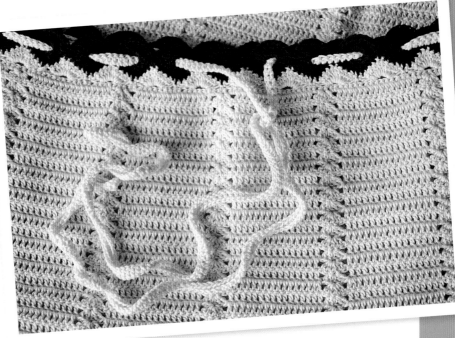

Knit Circle Skirt

Design by Gretchen Funk

The Knit Circle Skirt is created using a shell stitch pattern that closely mimics the look of the crocheted version. The knitted skirt has more flair than the original, and is every bit as lovely. This pattern calls for Berroco *Ultra Alpaca Fine*, which makes the knitting pure luxury.

Sizes

Woman's small (medium, large, extra-large)

Instructions are given for smallest size, with larger sizes in parentheses. When only 1 number is given, it applies to all sizes.

Finished Measurements

Waist circumference: 26½ (30, 33½, 37)"/ 67.5 (76, 85, 94)cm

Hip circumference: 35¼ (38¾, 42¼, 45¾"/ 89.5 (98.5, 107.5, 116)cm

Length: 22" (56cm), including crocheted waist and circles

Materials

- Berroco *Ultra Alpaca Fine* (fingering weight; 50% wool/20% superfine alpaca/30% nylon; 433 yd/400g per 3½ oz/100g skein): 4 (4, 5, 5) skeins Winter White #1201; 1 skein Pitch Black #1245
- Size 2 (2.75mm) 24" (60cm) and 32" (80cm) circular needles or size needed to obtain gauge
- Size D/3 (3.25mm) crochet hook
- Stitch markers, 1 in CC for beg of rnd
- Tapestry needle

Gauge

30 sts and 30 rnds = 4" (10cm) in garter st.

25 sts and 38 rnds = 4" (10cm) in pat st.

Adjust needle size as necessary to obtain correct gauge.

Special Abbreviations

Slip marker (sm): Slip marker when you come to it.

Increase 1 (Inc1): Make a backward loop and put on needle.

Rib Panel

Rnd 1: K1-tbl, *yo, k1-tbl; rep from * to marker.

Rnd 2: K1-tbl, *p3tog, k1-tbl; rep from * to marker.

Rep Rnds 1 and 2 for pat.

Pattern Notes

• This skirt is worked in the round from the waist down. The fabric is worked with WS facing (inside out) for easier knitting.

• The waistband and hem are crocheted to the body of the skirt after it is complete, following the instructions in the crocheted version of the skirt.

• The Shell and Rib panels alternate 11 times around. To make a larger or smaller skirt, cast on more or fewer stitches in increments of 11 stitches, adding/subtracting 1 stitch per incremental 11 stitches to the Rib section.

• A 12-round pattern repeat is worked 16 times; the shaping is done by increasing the number of stitches in the rib panel. To change the length or flare of the skirt, work more or fewer 12-round pattern repeats, working more or fewer increase rounds as desired.

• Change to longer circular needle when stitches no longer fit on 24" (60cm) needle.

Stitch Pattern

SHELL PANEL (6-st panel)

Rnd 1: P1-tbl, [p1, wrapping yarn around needle twice] 4 times, p1-tbl.

Rnd 2: P1-tbl, dropping extra loops and working in next 4 sts, [p4tog, k4tog] twice, p1-tbl.

Rnd 3: P1-tbl, yo, [p2tog] twice, yo, k1-tbl.

Rnd 4: P1-tbl, p4, p1-tbl.

Rep Rnds 1–4 for pat.

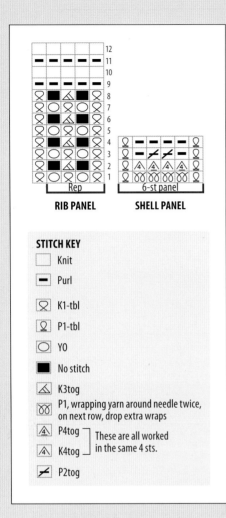

RIB PANEL

SHELL PANEL

STITCH KEY

- ☐ Knit
- ▬ Purl
- ⊠ K1-tbl
- ⊠ P1-tbl
- ○ YO
- ■ No stitch
- ◿ K3tog
- 凶 P1, wrapping yarn around needle twice, on next row, drop extra wraps
- ◿ P4tog ⎫ These are all worked
- ◿ K4tog ⎭ in the same 4 sts.
- ⤢ P2tog

Instructions

CO 165 (187, 209, 231) sts; pm for beg of rnd and join, taking care not to twist sts.

[Purl 1 rnd, knit 1 rnd] twice.

FIRST PATTERN REPEAT

Rnd 1 (set up pat): *Work Rnd 1 of Rib panel over 9 (11, 13, 15) sts, pm, work Shell panel over 6 sts, pm; rep from * around.

Rnds 2–8: Work 7 rnds even in est pat, ending with Rnd 8 of rib.

Rnd 9: *Purl to first marker, sm, work 6 sts in Shell panel, sm; rep from * around.

Rnd 10: *Knit to first marker, sm, work Shell panel, sm; rep from * around.

Rnds 11 and 12: Rep Rnds 9 and 10.

2ND REPEAT (inc)

Rnds 1–10: Work as for first rep.

Rnd 11 (Inc): *Inc1, purl to first marker, Inc1, sm, work Shell panel, sm; rep from * around—187 (209, 231, 253) sts with 11 (13, 15, 17) sts between rib markers.

Rnd 12: Rep Rnd 10.

3RD REPEAT

Rnd 1: *K1-tbl, work est rib to last st, k1-tbl, sm, work Shell panel, sm; rep from * around.

Rnds 2–8: Cont to work k1-tbl at beg and end of Rib panel, work even in est pat.

Rnds 9–12: Rep Rnds 9–12 of first rep.

4TH REPEAT (inc)

Rnds 1–10: Work as for 3rd rep.

Rnd 11: Work Inc rnd as for 2nd rep—209 (231, 253, 275) sts with 13 (15, 17, 19) sts between rib markers.

Rnd 12: Rep Rnd 10.

5TH REPEAT

Rnd 1: *Work Rnd 1 of Rib panel over to first marker, sm, work Shell panel; rep from * around.

Rnds 2–12: Work as for first rep.

6TH REPEAT (increase)

Work as for 2nd rep—231 (253, 275, 297) sts with 15 (17, 19, 21) sts between rib markers.

7TH REPEAT

Work as for 3rd rep.

8TH REPEAT (inc)
Work as for 4th rep—253 (275, 297, 319) sts with 17 (19, 21, 23) sts between rib markers.

9TH AND 10TH REPEATS
Work as for 5th rep.

11TH REPEAT (inc)
Work as for 2nd rep—275 (297, 319, 341) sts with 19 (21, 23, 25) sts between rib markers.

12TH AND 13TH REPEATS
Work as for 3rd rep.

14TH REPEAT (inc)
Work as for 4th rep—297 (319, 341, 363) sts with 21 (23, 25, 27) sts between rib markers.

15TH AND 16TH REPEATS
Work as for 5th rep, ending 16th rep on Rnd 8.

[Purl 1 rnd, knit 1 rnd] twice.

BO very loosely, using larger needle size if necessary.

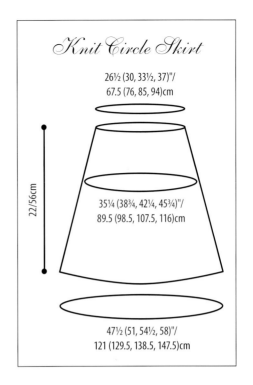

Knit Circle Skirt

26½ (30, 33½, 37)"/
67.5 (76, 85, 94)cm

22/56cm

35¼ (38¾, 42¼, 45¾)"/
89.5 (98.5, 107.5, 116)cm

47½ (51, 54½, 58)"/
121 (129.5, 138.5, 147.5)cm

Finishing

Turn skirt right side out.

Waistband
Rnd 1: With A, sc in each CO st around top; join with sl st to first st of rnd. Ch 1 and turn.

Continue working waistband as for crochet version of skirt.

Circle edging
With B, work as for crochet version of skirt. Make 47 (51, 54, 58) total circles without fastening off. Pin evenly spaced to bottom edge of skirt and, if necessary, add more circles or unravel extra ones; join first and last circles with sl st and fasten off. With B, sew to bottom of skirt.

Weave in all ends.

Drawstring
Work as for crochet version.

Block to finished measurements.

Evening Capelet

Design by Jennifer Hansen, Stitch Diva Studios

Think short, open poncho—a retro Hollywood glamour mini-cape for a very "now" sophisticated look. Just right to fight the nip in the air, this versatile flared capelet is the perfect shoulder-draping accent when you need just a little warmth with your style. Secured about the neck, the opening of this lovely capelet dramatically reveals the layer you're sporting beneath.

This classic little garment is knit in one piece from the top down and requires minimal finishing. Although engineered for mostly easy, autopilot stitching, this project does use one or two techniques that might teach you something, too. In addition to featuring a knit-in hem collar, it uses picked-up stitches for a snug ribbed collar, delicate yarnover increasing, and feminine short-row underlayers at each side.

Sizes

Woman's small (medium, large, extra-large) for circumference around bust and arms of 43 (47, 51, 56)"/109 (119.5, 129.5, 142)cm

Instructions are given for smallest size, with larger sizes in parentheses. When only 1 number is given, it applies to all sizes.

Finished Measurement

Length to neck: 17 (17½, 18, 18½)"/43 (44.5, 45.5, 47)cm

Materials

• Stitch Diva Studios *Studio Cashmere* (DK weight; 100% cashmere; 165 yd/150m per 1¾oz/50g skein): 4 (5, 6, 7) skeins Ruby

• Size 5 (3.75mm) needles

• Size 6 (4mm) 32" (80cm) circular needle or size needed to obtain gauge

• Spare circular needle, same size or smaller than circular needle

• Size D/3 (3.25mm) crochet hook

• 15 stitch markers

• One pair size #4 snaps (1 optional)

• One 1¾" (4.5cm) button

Gauge

19 sts and 25 rows = 4" (10cm) in St st with larger needle.

Adjust needle size as necessary to obtain correct gauge.

Special Abbreviation

W&T (Wrap and Turn): Slip next st pwise to RH needle, bring yarn around this st to RS, slip st back to LH needle, bring yarn back to WS, turn work to begin working back in the other direction. *To hide wraps:* On RS, ssk as follows: insert RH needle into front of wrap from bottom to top as if to knit, insert RH needle into st itself, knit both the wrap and st tog. On WS, p2tog as follows: with RH needle, pick up wrap from behind and place wrap fully (up and over) onto LH needle. Purl both the wrap and st together.

Special Techniques

Knit-in Hem: A knit-in hem is featured in this design to add stiffness at the neckline for closure. The hem requires use of a turning ridge, picking up sts with separate yarn, and 3-needle knitting to join the hem together. *For turning ridge:* Knit the sts through the back loops on the WS; this forms a purl ridge that creases the fabric on the RS.

Lifted Increase (Inc1): Turn the work slightly so that you can see the purl side of the next st. Insert RH needle from the top down into the purl bump that is directly below the st being worked on LH needle. Knit this st and then knit the st on the LH needle; 1 st is now 2.

Pattern Notes

• This capelet is worked from the top down.

• The 2 side "under-ruffles" are worked by picking up stitches between Secondary Increase Lines, then working short rows for a graceful downward curve.

• For a shorter or longer capelet, bind off on a nonincreasing RS row and pick up stitches between Secondary Increase Lines (see *Diagram*). Work ruffles to desired length following similar short-row shaping as written. If working short rows on a circular needle, hold shaping stitches on flexible portion of the needle to verify that the shaping works for your custom length.

Instructions

HEM
With larger needle, CO 83 (91, 99, 107) sts.

Beg with a WS row, work 4 rows St st.

Turning ridge (WS): K1-tbl across.

Work 4 rows St st.

Join hem (RS): Using a 3rd needle and separate yarn, leaving a 4" (10cm) tail, pick up (but do not knit) 83 (91, 99, 107) sts from cast-on row. Holding the 2 needles parallel with WS tog, knit first st on main needle tog with first st on spare needle; cont across working k2tog in this manner. Cut separate yarn, leaving a 4" (10cm) tail.

PRIMARY INCREASE LINE
Set-up row (WS): K4, pm, p15 (18, 20, 22), pm; [p22 (23, 25, 27), pm] twice; p16 (19, 21, 23), pm, k4.

Inc row (RS): K4, sm, Inc1; [knit to next marker, yo, sm, k1, yo] 3 times; knit to 1 st before last marker, Inc1, sm, k4—8 sts increased.

Maintaining 4-st garter edges and rem sts in St st, rep Inc row [every 4th row] 8 (9, 10, 12) times—155 (171, 187, 211) sts.

Work 1 WS row.

SECONDARY INCREASE LINE
Set-up row (RS): Slipping markers as you come to them, k19 (21, 23, 26), pm, Inc1, [k39 (43, 47, 53), pm, Inc1] 3 times, knit to end—159 (175, 191, 215) sts.

Work 1 row even.

Inc row (RS): K4, sm, Inc1, [knit to next marker, yo, sm, k1, yo] 7 times, knit to 1 st before last marker, Inc1, sm, k4—16 sts increased.

Maintaining est pat, rep Inc row [every 4th row] 4 (5, 6, 7) times—239 (271, 303, 343) sts.

Work 3 rows even and on last row, remove first and last markers.

TERTIARY INCREASE LINE
Set-up row (RS): Slipping markers as you come to them, [k13 (16, 18, 20), yo, pm, k1, yo, knit to marker, yo, sm, k1, yo] 7 times, k13 (16, 18, 20), yo, pm, k1, yo, knit to end—269 (301, 333, 373) sts.

Work 3 rows even.

Inc row (RS): Knit to first marker, [yo, sm, k1, yo, knit to next marker] 14 times, yo, sm, k1, yo, knit to end—30 sts increased.

Maintaining pat as est, work Inc row [every 4th row] 4 (4, 5, 6) times—419 (451, 513, 583) sts.

Work 1 WS row.

DECORATIVE EYELETS (no further incs)

Eyelet row (RS): [Knit to 2 sts before marker, k2tog, yo, sm, k1, yo, k2tog] 15 times, knit to end.

Maintaining pat as est, rep Eyelet row [every 4th row] twice.

Work 1 WS row.

Knit 4 rows.

Bind off kwise on RS.

COLLAR

With RS facing and using smaller needle, pick up and knit 82 (90, 98, 106) sts along turning ridge.

Row 1 (WS): K4, *p2, k2; rep from * to last 6 sts, p2, k4.

Row 2: K4, *k2, p2; rep from * to last 6 sts, k6.

Rep Rows 1 and 2 until collar measures approx 3½" (9cm).

Bind off loosely in rib.

UNDER-RUFFLES

With WS facing and cape turned upside down, pick up all sts (but do not work) along the purl bumps of 7th row from the lower edge (the knit row between last sets of eyelets) between the 2 Secondary Increase Lines on one side as pictured in Diagram A. When picking up the sts, place 3 markers to match positions of knit sts between eyelets on main fabric. Join yarn.

Row 1 (WS): Purl to last 8 (10, 11, 12) sts, W&T.

Row 2: Establish Eyelet row and work to last 8 (10, 11, 12) sts, W&T.

Row 3: Purl to 8 (10, 11, 12) sts before previous wrap, W&T.

Row 4: Knit to 8 (10, 11, 12) sts before previous wrap, W&T.

Row 5: Purl to 5 (5, 5, 6) sts before previous wrap, W&T.

Row 6: Work est Eyelet row to 5 (5, 5, 6) sts before previous wrap, W&T.

Row 7: Purl to 2 (2, 2, 3) sts before previous wrap, W&T.

Row 8: Knit to 2 (2, 2, 3) sts before previous wrap, W&T.

Row 9: Purl to end, hiding wraps as you come to them.

Row 10: Work est Eyelet row to end, hiding wraps.

Row 11: Purl across.

Next 4 rows: Knit.

BO kwise on RS.

Finishing

Weave in all ends. Block piece to minimize curling at hem.

Closure
Sew button just above Primary Increase Line at the knitted-in hem.

Make Button Loop: With crochet hook, attach yarn with slip st at RS of top edge of opposite hem; ch 16, sl st to bottom edge of hem, turn.

Work about 24 sc in the ch 16 space, sl st to opposite edge of garment, make one sc in each sc on button loop, sl st to opposite side of garment.

Tie off & weave in ends.

Inner closure (optional): We recommend that the inner edge of the capelet be secured to the inner neckline of the capelet with a snap closure (see *Diagram*). With yarn, sew on snap closures.

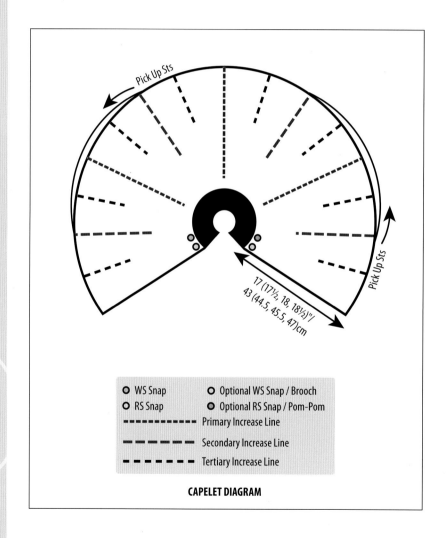

CAPELET DIAGRAM

○ WS Snap	○ Optional WS Snap / Brooch
○ RS Snap	○ Optional RS Snap / Pom-Pom
- - - - - - -	Primary Increase Line
— — — —	Secondary Increase Line
■ — ■ — ■	Tertiary Increase Line

Diagram labels: Pick Up Sts, Pick Up Sts, 17 (17½, 18, 18½)"/ 43 (44.5, 45.5, 47)cm

Moss Rose Brooch

Design by Nora J. Bellows

Sometimes a sweater, coat, or hat just needs a touch of vintage romance, and that's exactly what the Moss Rose Brooch provides. Felt this lovely flower or leave it alone. We've provided instructions for both.

Materials

VERSION 1 (unfelted)
- Tilli Tomas *Flurries* (worsted weight; 80% merino wool/20% beads; 70 yd/64m per 1¾ oz/50g ball): 1 ball each Ruby Wine (A), Raspberry (B), Coral Sap (C), Hope (D), Natural (E)

- Size 9 (5.5mm) needles

- Tapestry needle

VERSION 2 (felted)
- Stonehedge Fiber Mill *Shepherd's Wool* (worsted weight; 100% merino wool; 250 yd/229m per 3½ oz/100g skein): 1 skein each Peaches & Cream (A), Peach (B), Antique Rose (C), Christmas Red (D), Garnet (E)

- Size 11 (8mm) needles

- Tapestry needle

- 2mm seed beads for petals and flower center (optional)

- Pin back

Gauge

Gauge is not critical for this project.

- This flower is made in 1 piece, composed of a series of 28 petals of diminishing size, each of which is connected to the previous one. There are 5 [6-st] petals, 5 [5-st] petals, 10 [4-st] petals, 5 [3-st] petals, and 3 [2-st] petals.

- Each petal is worked in 2 halves using short rows. Do not wrap the last stitch before turning; this will make desired holes down the center of the petals.

- Work unfelted flower with a single strand of yarn.

- Work felted flower with a double strand of yarn.

- If used in different color combinations, the listed yarns will make 6–8 unfelted flowers and 7–9 felted flowers.

Instructions

With A (single strand for unfelted version, double strand for felted version) and appropriate needle size, using cable method, CO 6 sts.

6-ST PETALS (5)

*Row 1 (RS): K1f&b, k4; turn, leaving 1 st unworked—7 sts on needles.

Row 2: P6.

Rep [Rows 1 and 2] 5 times, leaving 1 more st unworked each RS row—12 sts.

Next row (RS): K2tog, k5 (working first previously unworked st), turn—11 sts on needles.

Next row: P6.

Rep last 2 rows 4 times, then work RS row once more—6 sts on needle.

Connect to next petal as follows:

Row 1 (WS): [P2tog] 3 times—3 sts.

Row 2: [K1f&b] 3 times—6 sts.

Row 3: P6.

Rep from * until 5 petals are complete, ending last petal before working connecting rows.

5-ST PETALS (5)

Change to B. Connect to previous petal as follows:

Row 1 (WS): [P2tog] 3 times—3 sts.

Row 2 (RS): [K1f&b] twice, k1—5 sts.

Row 3: P5.

Work petal in same manner as 6-st petals as follows:

Row 4 (RS): K1f&b, k3; turn, leaving 1 st unworked—6 sts.

Row 5: P5.

Rep [Rows 4 and 5] 4 times—10 sts.

Next row (RS): K2tog, k4 (working first previously unworked st), turn—9 sts.

Next row: P5.

Rep last 2 rows 3 times, then work RS row once more—5 sts.

Connect to next petal as follows:

Row 1 (WS): P1, [p2tog] twice—3 sts.

Row 2: [K1f&b] twice, k1—5 sts.

Row 3: P5.

Rep from Row 4 until 5 [5-st] petals are complete, ending last petal before working connecting rows.

4-ST PETALS (10)

Change to C. Connect to previous petal as follows:

Row 1 (WS): P1, [p2tog] twice—3 sts.

Row 2 (RS): K1f&b, K2—4 sts.

Row 3: P4.

Work petal in same manner as previous petals as follows:

Row 4: K1f&b, k2; turn, leaving 1 st unworked—5 sts on needles.

Row 5: P4.

Rep [Rows 4 and 5] 3 times—8 sts.

Next row (RS): K2tog, k3 (working first previously unworked st), turn—7 sts.

Next row: P4.

Rep last 2 rows twice, then work RS row once more—4 sts.

Connect to next petal as follows:

Row 1 (WS): [P2tog] twice—2 sts.

Row 2: [K1f&b] twice—4 sts.

Row 3: P4.

Rep from Row 4 until 10 [4-st] petals are complete, ending last petal before working connecting rows.

3-ST PETALS (5)

Change to D. Connect to previous petal as follows:

Row 1 (WS): [P2tog] twice—2 sts.

Row 2: K1f&b, k1—3 sts.

Row 3: P3.

Work petal in same manner as previous petals as follows:

Row 4: K1f&b, k1, turn—4 sts on needles.

Row 5: P3.

Rep [Rows 4 and 5] twice—6 sts.

Next row (RS): K2tog, k2 (working first previously unworked st), turn—5 sts.

Next row: P3.

Rep last 2 rows once, then work RS row once more—3 sts.

Connect to next petal as follows:

Row 1 (WS): P1, p2tog—2 sts.

Row 2: K1f&b, K1—3 sts.

Row 3: P3.

Rep from Row 4 until 5 [3-st] petals are complete, ending last petal before working connecting rows.

2-ST PETALS (3)

Change to E. Connect to previous petal as follows:

> **Row 1 (WS):** P1, p2tog—2 sts.
>
> **Row 2:** K2.
>
> **Row 3:** P2.

Work petal in same manner as previous petals as follows:

> **Row 4:** K1f&b, turn—3 sts on needles.
>
> **Row 5:** P2.
>
> **Rows 6 and 7:** Rep Rows 4 and 5—4 sts.
>
> **Row 8:** K2tog, k1 (working first previously unworked st), turn—3 sts.
>
> **Row 9:** P2.
>
> **Row 10:** Rep Row 8—2 sts.

Connect to next petal as follows:

> **Row 11:** P2tog—1 st.
>
> **Row 12:** K1f&b—2 sts.
>
> **Row 13:** P2.

Rep Rows 4–13 once, then work Rows 4–10.

BO rem 2 sts.

Cut yarn leaving a long tail (use this tail for assembling the rose).

Finishing

For unfelted rose, weave in ends.

For felted rose, ends can be left about 3" (7.5cm) long and cut off *after* felting.

Assemble rose

Once finished, the petals will look as though they are all strung on a line. Lay petals out flat, then begin to form flower. Starting with the smallest petals at center and working out, wrap petals around center in a spiral, RS facing in. Using yarn and a tapestry needle, secure the flower by stitching through all layers at center, drawing the center together as you go.

Felting instructions

After petals are sewn in place, the flower is ready for felting (if desired). For best results, felt in a top-loading washer set on smallest load size and hottest water setting. Rather than letting the machine go through multiple cycles, turn back the dial and let items agitate longer. Felt flowers in lingerie bags or pillow protectors to minimize fuzziness. Reshaping flowers midway through felting helps blocking later. Flowers achieve a soft felt in approximately two agitation cycles. Because a soft felt is preferable, stitches may still be slightly visible. Check your flowers often while felting so they do not felt hard. A machine rinse is not advised. More agitation may cause flowers to felt too hard. Remove softly felted flowers from washer and rinse by hand, squeezing out excess water. Air dry or spin-dry in the machine.

Blocking felted flower

Blocking should not be neglected. Unblocked flowers will not have the cuplike shape featured in this pattern. Unfelted flower petals tend to curl backward. Once felted, petals may still curl backward unless you pull each petal forward using your thumb on RS, and your fingers on WS. Help flowers retain this shape by placing them close together or in large muffin tins while they dry.

Sew pin back to back of felted flower.

Embellish felted flower with seed beads as desired.

Lotus Pullover

Design by Teva Durham

Barbara Walker writes that the Lotus Stitch hails from Japan. There is certainly some excellent crafting emerging from Japan to this day, and notably the Zakka movement. In Zakka, humble materials or kitschy objects lend exquisite style. The Lotus Stitch's stylized floral repeats appear rather primitive, like a woodcut print, and at the same time very sophisticated. The arrangement has a plaidlike element, having both strong vertical and horizontal lines. I have paired the lotus pattern with a rib pattern that aligns and emphasizes the vertical ridges in the lace. I have selected dusty colors for a vintage look. In this version, I have kept the two colors separate—using the camel color only for the trim. But the pattern could be adapted to include the trim color in contrast stripes on the rows with purl ridges or even with separate blocks of color for each tier of lotus flowers.

Sizes

Woman's small (medium, large, extra-large, 2X-large)

Instructions are given for smallest size, with larger sizes in parentheses. When only 1 number is given, it applies to all sizes.

Finished Measurements

Bust: 32 (36, 40, 44, 48)"/81.5 (91.5, 101.5, 112, 122)cm

Length: 22¾ (23¼, 23¾, 24¾, 25¼)"/58 (59, 60.5, 63, 64)cm

Materials **3**

- Loop-d-Loop by Teva Durham *Moss* (DK weight; 85% extra-fine merino wool/15% nylon; 163 yd/147m per 1¾oz/50g ball): 2 (3, 3, 3, 4) balls Camel #09 (A) and 5 (6, 6, 7, 7) balls Lt. Lilac #05 (B)
- Size 6 (4mm) needles size needed to obtain gauge
- Spare needle or stitch holder
- Smooth fine-gauge waste yarn
- Tapestry needle

Gauge

20 sts and 26 rows = 4" (10cm) in Lotus pat [each 16-row rep = 2½" (6.5cm)]

21 sts and 26 rows = 4" (10cm) in 3x1 Slipped Rib

21 sts and 26 rows = 4" (10cm) in 4x1 Slipped Rib

Adjust needle size as necessary to obtain correct gauge.

CDD (Centered Double Dec): *On RS:* slip 2 sts as if to k2tog, k1, pass slipped sts over; *on WS:* slip 2 sts, 1 at a time kwise; pass these sts to the LH needle in their twisted position; insert RH needle through the backs of these 2 sts as if to p2tog-tbl and slip off LH needle; p1, psso.

M1L (Make 1 Left): Insert LH needle from front to back under the running thread between the last st worked and next st on LH needle; knit into the back of resulting loop.

M1R (Make 1 Right): Insert LH needle from back to front under the running thread between the last st worked and next st on LH needle. With RH needle, knit into the front of resulting loop.

Special Technique

Tubular cast-on: With smooth fine-gauge waste yarn and using backward-loop method, cast on half the total number of sts required +1. With A, purl 1 row, knit 1 row, purl 1 row, knit 1 row. *Joining row:* P1 from RH needle, *dive down with LH needle and pick up first purl bump A from cast-on row (go into the st from top to bottom), then knit this st tbl, p1 from LH needle; rep from * to end.

Pattern Notes

• This sweater is designed for a very close fit—it has no ease.

• If making your sweater with the tighter waistband, start with the tubular cast-on—this will give the bottom edge enough elasticity to get over your head.

• When shaping in Lotus pattern, remember that decreases and yarnovers must be paired to maintain pattern stitch count. If you cannot work both elements of a pair, then work the stitches in St st.

Stitch Pattern

LOTUS PATTERN (multiple of 10 sts + 1)
Rows 1–5: Knit.

Row 6 (WS): P1, *yo, p3, CDD, p3, yo, p1; rep from *.

Row 7: K2, *yo, k2, CDD, k2, yo, k3; rep from *, end last rep k2.

Row 8: P3, *yo, p1, CDD, p1, yo, p5; rep from *, end last rep p3.

Row 9: K4, *yo, CDD, yo, k7; rep from *, end last rep k4.

Row 10: P2, *k2, p3; rep from *, end last rep p2.

Row 11: K1, *yo, ssk, p1, yo, CDD, p1, k2tog, yo, k1; rep from *.

Row 12: P3, *k1, p3, k1, p5; rep from *, end last rep p3.

Row 13: K2, *yo, ssk, yo, CDD, yo, k2tog, yo, k3; rep from *, end last rep k2.

Row 14: P2, *k1, p5, k1, p3; rep from *, end last rep p2.

Row 15: K2, *p1, k1, yo, CDD, yo, k1, p1, k3; rep from *, end last rep k2.

Row 16: P2, *k1, p5, k1, p3; rep from *, end last rep p2.

Rep Rows 1–16 for pat.

3X1 SLIPPED RIB
Row 1 (RS): Sl 1, *p3, k1; rep from * to end.

Row 2: *Sl 1, k3; rep from * to last st, p1.

Rep Rows 1 and 2 for pat.

4X1 SLIPPED RIB
Row 1 (RS): Sl 1, *p4, k1; rep from to end.

Row 2: Sl 1, k4; rep from * to last st, p1.

Rep Rows 1 and 2 for pat.

Instructions

BACK
Waistband
With A, using tubular method for elasticity, CO 65 (73, 81, 89, 97) sts.

Work in 3x1 Slipped Rib for 4"/10cm, ending with a WS row.

Inc row (RS): Sl 1, *p1, p1f&b, p1, k1; rep from * to end—81 (91, 101, 111, 121) sts.

[If a looser-fitting waistband is desired, CO 81 (91, 101, 111, 121) sts; work in 4x1 Slipped Rib for 4" (10cm), ending with a WS row.]

Body
Cut A. Join B and purl 1 row.

Work even in Lotus pat until piece measures 14" (35.5cm), ending with a WS row.

Shape armholes

Next 2 rows: BO 3 (5, 5, 5, 8) sts, work in pat to end—75 (81, 91, 101, 105) sts.

Dec row (RS): K1, ssk, work in est pat to last 3 sts, k2tog, k1—73 (79, 89, 99, 103) sts.

Maintaining pat, rep Dec row [every RS row] 1 (4, 4, 4, 6) times—71 (71, 81, 91, 91) sts.

Work even until 5 (5, 5, 6, 6) total reps of Lotus pat are complete, then work Rows 1–5 once more.

Cut B. Join A and purl 1 row.

Work even in 4x1 Slipped Rib until armholes measure 7½ (8, 8½, 9½, 10)".

Shape shoulders

BO 6 sts at beg of next 4 rows, 3 (3, 4, 5, 5) sts at beg of following 4 rows, then BO rem 35 (35, 41, 47, 47) back neck sts.

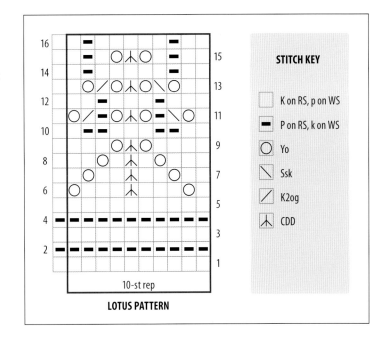

STITCH KEY

☐	K on RS, p on WS
▬	P on RS, k on WS
○	Yo
╲	Ssk
╱	K2og
人	CDD

10-st rep

LOTUS PATTERN

FRONT

Work as for back until armholes measure 5 (5½, 6, 7, 7½)".

Divide for front neck

Mark center st.

Next row (RS): Work in pat to 2 sts before marked center st, p2tog, knit center st; place next 35 (35, 40, 40, 45) sts on holder or spare needle for right front.

Left front neck and shoulder

Work 1 WS row, adjusting for neck dec as follows on all succeeding WS rows: knit the knits and slip the purl sts as they appear.

Cont in est rib and dec at beg of RS rows only as follows:

Dec row 1: Work in pat to last 4 sts, p1, p2tog, k1—34 (34, 39, 39, 44) sts.

Dec row 2: Work in pat to last 3 sts, p2tog, k1—33 (33, 38, 38, 43) sts.

Dec row 3: Work in pat to last 2 sts, k2tog—32 (32, 37, 37, 42) sts.

Dec row 4: Work in pat to last 2 sts, k2tog—31 (31, 37, 37, 41) sts.

Dec row 5: Work in pat to last 5 sts, p2, p2tog, k1—30 (30, 36, 36, 40, 40) sts.

Dec row 6: Work in pat to last 5 sts, p2, p2tog, k1—29 (29, 35, 35, 39) sts.

Work even until armhole measures 7½ (8, 8½, 9½, 10)", ending with a WS row.

Next 4 RS rows: Bind off 6 sts at shoulder edge twice, then 3 (3, 4, 5, 5) sts twice—11 (11, 15, 15, 17) sts rem at neck edge.

Work 1 WS row, then BO.

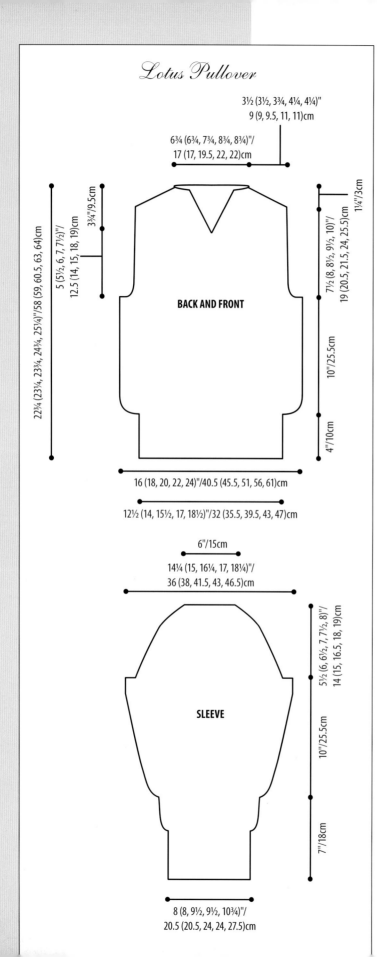

Lotus Pullover

BACK AND FRONT

3½ (3½, 3¾, 4¼, 4¼)"
9 (9, 9.5, 11, 11)cm

6¾ (6¾, 7¾, 8¾, 8¾)"/
17 (17, 19.5, 22, 22)cm

3¾"/9.5cm

5 (5½, 6, 7, 7½)"/
12.5 (14, 15, 18, 19)cm

22¾ (23¼, 23¾, 24¾, 25¼)"/58 (59, 60.5, 63, 64)cm

7½ (8, 8½, 9½, 10)"/
19 (20.5, 21.5, 24, 25.5)cm

1¼"/3cm

10"/25.5cm

4"/10cm

16 (18, 20, 22, 24)"/40.5 (45.5, 51, 56, 61)cm

12½ (14, 15½, 17, 18½)"/32 (35.5, 39.5, 43, 47)cm

SLEEVE

6"/15cm

14¼ (15, 16¼, 17, 18¼)"/
36 (38, 41.5, 43, 46.5)cm

5½ (6, 6½, 7, 7½, 8)"/
14 (15, 16.5, 18, 19)cm

10"/25.5cm

7"/18cm

8 (8, 9½, 9½, 10¾)"/
20.5 (20.5, 24, 24, 27.5)cm

Right front neck and shoulder

Slip right front sts to needle with RS facing; join A to neck edge.

Next row (RS): Pick up and knit 1 st into center neck st, p2tog, work in est pat to end—35 (35, 40, 40, 45) sts.

Cont as for left front reversing neck and shoulder shaping.

SLEEVE
Cuff

With A and using tubular method, CO 41 (41, 49, 49, 57) sts.

Work in 3x1 Slipped Rib for 4" (10cm), ending with a WS row.

Inc row (RS): Sl 1, *p1, p1f&b, p1, k1; rep from * to end—51 (51, 61, 61, 71) sts.

Work in 4x1 Slipped Rib until piece measures 7" (18cm), ending with a RS row.

BODY

Cut A. Join B and purl 1 row.

Work 6 (4, 6, 4, 4) rows in Lotus pat.

Inc row (RS): K1, M1R, work in est pat to last st, M1L, k1—53 (53, 63, 63, 73) sts.

Working new sts into pat as they accumulate (see Pattern Note), rep Inc row [every 6 (4, 6, 4, 6) rows] 9 (6, 9, 6, 9) times, then [every — (6, —, 6 —) rows] — (5, —, 5, —) times—71 (75, 81, 85, 91) sts.

Work even until sleeve measures approx 17", ending with the same pat row as for back before starting armhole shaping (this is to match up pat across sleeve seam).

SHAPE SLEEVE CAP

Next 2 rows: BO 3 (5, 5, 5, 8) sts, work in pat to end—65 (65, 71, 75, 75) sts.

Dec row (RS): K1, ssk, work in est pat to last 3 sts, k2tog, k1—63 (63, 69, 73, 73) sts.

Maintaining pat, rep Dec row [every RS row] 6 times—51 (51, 57, 61, 61) sts.

Work 2 (4, 2, 4, 6) rows even, ending with a WS row.

Rep Dec row [every RS row] 10 (10, 13, 15, 15) times—31 sts.

Finishing

Weave in ends. Block to finished measurements.

Sew shoulder seams.

Set in sleeves as follows: measure 2" (5cm) down from each shoulder seam and mark; gather top cap, which measures approx 6" (15cm) across, and sew between markers; ease in rest of cap.

Sew side and sleeve seams.

Sporty Polo Sweater

Design by Andrea M. Holliger

This blouse is adapted from a vintage *Vogue* dress pattern that appeared just after World War II. Patterns from this time feature many Japanese influences, as you can see here in the kimono sleeves.

Size

To fit bust size 30 (34, 38, 42, 46)"/76 (86.5, 96.5, 106.5, 117)cm

Instructions are given for smallest size, with larger sizes in parentheses. When only 1 number is given, it applies to all sizes.

Finished Measurements

Circumference: 29½ (34, 37, 41, 45)"/76 (86.5, 94, 104, 114.5)cm

Length: 22¼" (56.5cm)

Materials

• Caron *Spa* (sport weight; 75% microdenier acrylic/25% rayon from bamboo; 251 yd/230m per 3 oz/85g ball): 6 (6, 7, 9, 10) balls Soft Sunshine #0003

• Size 4 (3.5mm) needles

• Size 6 (4mm) needles or size needed to obtain gauge

• Size F/5 (3.75mm) crochet hook

• Stitch holder (optional)

• 5 buttons

• Tapestry needle

• Pearlized belt closure

Gauge

31 sts and 40 rows = 4" (10cm) in pat st.

Adjust needle size as necessary to obtain correct gauge.

TAILORED BLOUSE—NO. 120

This typifies the mode for the shirt-maker blouse to be worn with suits and sport skirts. The illustrated blouse is made of Ecru Mercerized Crochet Size 5. It is equally smart in White. The buttons may match or add a touch of color to harmonize with skirt or hat.

M1L (Make 1 Left): Insert LH needle from front to back under the running thread between the last st worked and next st on LH needle; knit into the back of resulting loop.

M1R (Make 1 Right): Insert LH needle from back to front under the running thread between the last st worked and next st on LH needle. With RH needle, knit into the front of resulting loop.

Stitch Pattern

VERTICAL SLIP ST STRIPES
(multiple of 4 sts + 3)
Row 1 (RS): K3, *sl 1, k3; rep from * to end.

Row 2: Purl.

Rep Rows 1 and 2 for pat.

Instructions

BACK
With smaller needles, CO 115 (131, 143, 159, 175) sts.

Row 1 (RS): K1, *p1, k1; rep from * to end.

Work 7 rows in est rib.

Switch to larger needles and work Vertical Slip St Stripe pat until body measures 15" or desired length to armholes, ending with a WS row.

Increase for sleeve
Inc row (RS): K1, M1R, work in pat to last st, M1L, k1—117 (133, 145, 161, 177) sts.

Working new sts into pat as they accumulate, rep Inc row [every RS row] 6 (6, 9, 12, 15) times—129 (145, 163, 185, 207) sts.

Work even until sleeve measures 6¼" (16cm) from first inc.

Shape shoulder
BO 5 (6, 7, 8, 9) sts at beg of next 4 (8, 10, 10, 8) rows—109 (97, 93, 105, 135) sts.

BO 6 (7, 8, 9, 10) sts at beg of next 10 (6, 4, 4, 6) rows.

BO rem 49 (55, 61, 69, 75) sts for back neck.

FRONT
Work as for back to sleeve inc.

Divide for placket
Slip 61 (69, 75, 83, 91) sts on left half of piece to waste yarn or holder for left front.

Right side
Increase for sleeve
Next row (RS): K1, M1R, work in pat across rem 53 (61, 67, 75, 83) sts, CO 7 sts for buttonband (worked in St st)—62 (70, 76, 84, 92) sts.

Cont to inc 1 st at sleeve edge [every RS row] 6 (6, 9, 12, 15) times—68 (76, 85, 96, 107) sts, working new sts into pat as they accumulate.

Work even until sleeve measures 6¼" (16cm) from first inc, ending with a RS row.

Shape neck and shoulder

Next row (WS): BO 14 (17, 13, 17, 13) sts at neck edge, work to end—54 (59, 72, 79, 94) sts.

BO 2 (2, 3, 3, 4) sts at neck edge [every WS row] 7 times.

At the same time, BO 5 (6, 7, 8, 9) sts at shoulder edge [every RS row] 2 (4, 5, 5, 4) times, then 6 (7, 8, 9, 10) sts at shoulder edge [every RS row] 5 (3, 2, 2, 3) times.

Place markers for 5 evenly spaced buttons on buttonband.

Left side

Move 61 (69, 75, 83, 91) sts from holder onto needle.

On left side, work buttonholes 3 sts from placket edge to correspond with placement of markers as follows: On first row, BO 2 sts; on next row, CO 2 sts over bound-off sts.

At the same time, shape sleeve as follows:

Increase for sleeve

Next row (RS): Work in pat to last st, M1L, k1—62 (70, 76, 84, 92) sts.

Cont to inc 1 st at sleeve edge [every RS row] 6 (6, 9, 12, 15) times—68 (76, 85, 96, 107) sts, working new sts into pat as they accumulate.

Work even until sleeve measures 6¼" (16cm) from first inc, ending with a WS row.

Shape neck and shoulder

Next row (RS): BO 14 (17, 13, 17, 13) sts at neck edge, work to end—54 (59, 72, 79, 94) sts.

BO 2 (2, 3, 3, 4) sts at neck edge [every RS row] 7 times.

At the same time, BO 5 (6, 7, 8, 9) sts at shoulder edge [every WS row] 2 (4, 5, 5, 4) times, then 6 (7, 8, 9, 10) sts at shoulder edge [every WS row] 5 (3, 2, 2, 3) times.

COLLAR

CO 103 (115, 133, 151, 163) sts.

Purl 1 row.

Set-up and inc row (RS): K1, M1R, k4, *sl 1, k3; rep from * to last 2 sts, k1, M1L, k1—105 (117, 135, 153, 165) sts.

Working new sts into est pat as they accumulate, inc 1 st each end [every RS row] 3 more times—111 (123, 141, 159, 171) sts.

Work even until piece measures 1½" (4cm), ending with a RS row.

Dec row (WS): *P4, p2tog, repeat from *, end p3—93 (103, 118, 133, 143) sts

Bind off rem sts.

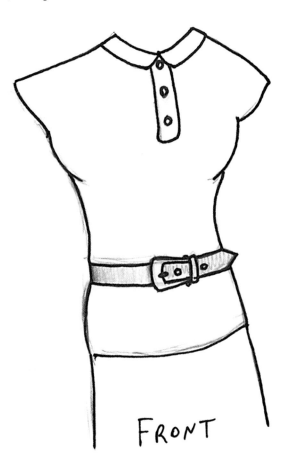

FRONT

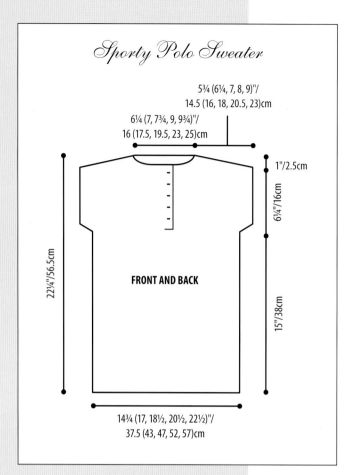

Sporty Polo Sweater

5¾ (6¼, 7, 8, 9)"/
14.5 (16, 18, 20.5, 23)cm

6¼ (7, 7¾, 9, 9¾)"/
16 (17.5, 19.5, 23, 25)cm

1"/2.5cm

6¼"/16cm

22¼"/56.5cm

15"/38cm

FRONT AND BACK

14¾ (17, 18½, 20½, 22½)"/
37.5 (43, 47, 52, 57)cm

BELT
CO 14 sts.

Work in St st for 30" (76cm) or desired length.

BO.

Finishing

Weave in all ends.

Block pieces to finished measurements.

Sew shoulder and side seams; do not sew underarm sleeve seam.

Sew on collar; tack down collar edge as necessary.

Sew on buttons.

Attach belt closure.

Work 1 row sc around collar and sleeve edge.

Belt loops
If desired, make belt loops as follows: Put on sweater and mark natural waist at sides. With crochet hook, at marked positions, pull yarn from WS to RS and make a chain long enough to hold belt; fasten off and pull yarn back to WS. Weave in both ends.

Vintage Belts

Designs by MaryJane Butters

A belt is a great final touch to an outfit, as any lady knew in the 1940s. These 1940s crocheted belts have been adapted for knitting and crochet, retaining the neat texture and rigidity of the crocheted rounds and medallions and infusing the belts with a knitted contrast. The colors and materials are also contemporary, using cotton with hemp cord accents to give it a natural and "green" connection.

Materials (all belts)

- J&P Coats *Royale* (100% cotton crochet thread size 3, 150 yd/137m per ball): See each pattern for specifics
- Size 6 (4mm) double-pointed needles or size needed to obtain gauge
- Size 6 (4mm) 29" (80cm) circular needle or size needed to obtain gauge
- Size G/6 (4mm) crochet hook
- Tapestry needle

Gauge (all belts)

17 sts and 32 rows= 4" (10cm) in garter st with 3 strands held tog.

16 sts and 14 rows= 4" (10cm) in single crochet with 3 strands held tog.

Adjust needle size as necessary to obtain correct gauge.

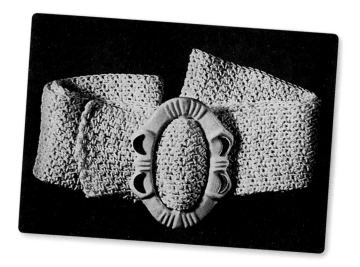

Pattern Note

All belts are worked with 3 strands of crochet thread size 3 held together.

Tip: To mark the beginning of rounds while crocheting, put a piece of waste yarn in a contrasting color across the top of the stitches after you join rounds and before you begin the next round. You can easily pull it out after you finish the round and replace for next round.

Finished Measurements

Width: 2" (5cm)

Length: as desired

Materials

• J&P Coats *Royale*: 2 balls Black #12 (A), 1 ball Scarlet #6 (B)

• One ⅝" (1.5cm) flat button

Instructions

BELT

With 3 strands A held tog, CO 10 sts.

Knit every row until belt measures desired length.

BO.

Weave in ends.

Circle trim

With 1 strand A and 2 strands B held tog and using crochet hook, ch 4, join to first ch with sl st to form ring, pm, ch 1.

Rnd 1: Sc 10 into the center of the ring, join to previous rnd with sl st, pm, ch 1—10 sc.

Rnd 2: 2 sc in each sc, join to previous rnd with sl st, pm, ch 1—20 sc.

Rnd 3: Sc in each sc, join to previous rnd with sl st, pm, ch 1.

Rnd 4: *Sc in first sc, 2 sc in 2nd sc; rep from * 9 times, join to previous rnd with sl st, ch 1—30 sc.

Fasten off. Weave in ends with tapestry needle.

Finishing

Sew the circle to the center of the belt.

With crochet hook and 1 strand of A, make a chain for a button loop in center of one end of the belt.

Weave in ends.

Sew button to inside of the belt at other end so it doesn't show.

Medallion Belt

Finished Measurements

Medallion diameter: approx 3¾" (9.5cm)

Belt length: 27 (30, 33)"/68.5 (76, 84)cm

Materials

• J&P Coats *Royale* 2 (2, 3) balls in Coffee #365 (A)

• All-natural 20-lb hemp twine (100% hemp; 400 ft/366m per 3½ oz/100g)

Instructions

Medallions
Make 9 (10, 11)

Using crochet hook and 3 strands A held tog, ch 10, join to first ch with sl st to form ring, ch 1.

Rnd 1: Sc 10 times into the center of the ring; join to previous rnd with sl st, pm, ch 1—10 sc.

Rnd 2: 2 sc in each sc around; join to previous rnd with sl st, pm, ch 1—20 sc.

Rnd 3: Sc in each sc around; join to previous rnd with sl st, pm, ch 1.

Rnd 4: *Sc in first sc, 2 sc in 2nd sc; rep from * around; join to previous rnd with sl st, pm, ch 1—30 sc.

Rnd 5: Sc in each sc around; join to previous rnd with sl st.

Cut yarn and weave in ends with tapestry needle.

Overlap edges of medallions about ½" (1.25cm) and sew in place at 2 points on the edges. Be careful to only sew on outer edges so that the cord tie can thread through between medallions and through the medallion centers.

I-Cord Tie
With dpn and 2 strands of B held tog, CO 5 sts.

*K5, do not turn; slip sts back to LH; rep from *, pulling cord tight across the back at beg of each row until I-cord measures 12" (30.5cm) longer than the medallion belt.

K5tog, then fasten off. Weave tails into center of cord.

Weave cord through center hole of first medallion, then through slot opening between first and second medallions; continue to weave cord in this manner to end. Tie in front to close belt.

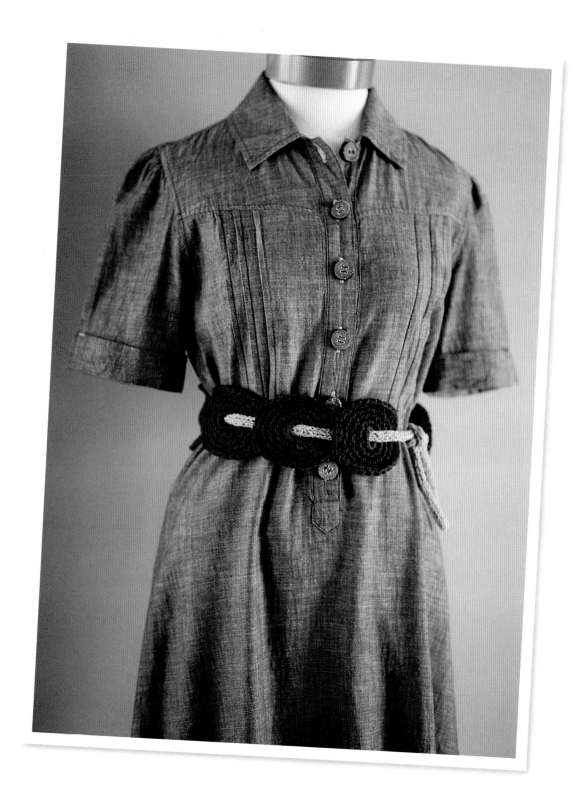

Bow Belt

Finished Measurements

Width: 2" (5cm)

Length: 28 (30, 32, 34)"/71 (76, 81.5, 86.5)cm

Materials

• J&P Coats *Royale*: 1 (2, 2, 2) balls black #12 (A); 1 ball warm teal #65 (B)

• One ⅝" (1.5cm) flat button

• 18" (46cm) black velvet ribbon, ⅝" (1.5cm) wide

Instructions

Belt
With 3 strands A held tog, CO 118 (127, 135, 143) sts.

Knit 14 rows.

BO all sts.

Bow Pieces (make 2)
With 3 strands B held tog, CO 19 sts.

Knit 28 rows.

Dec row: K1, k2tog, knit to end—18 sts.

Rep Dec row [every 3 rows] 4 times, then [every row] 9 times—5 sts.

Bind off row: K2tog, k1, BO first st, k2tog, BO 1, fasten off last st.

Weave in ends.

Finishing

Place one of the bow pieces at one end of the belt, the narrow side extending beyond about ½" (1.25cm), so that the end of the black belt does not show on the right side. Sew in place. Rep for the other bow piece on the other end of the belt.

With crochet hook and 1 strand of A, make a short chain for a button loop in center of one end of the belt.

Weave in ends.

Sew button to inside of the belt at other end, making sure that it doesn't show.

Fold ribbon so that it is half its original width and machine-sew along the edge. Tie in a bow and sew onto the side of the bow piece that's covering the button loop so it looks centered when the belt is buttoned.

Charming Shoulderette

Design by Betty Christiansen

Adapted from a knitted baby shrug made in the 1930s (bottom right), this shoulderette is completely adult and modern, with just a hint of old-fashioned appeal lent by a garter eyelet stitch pattern and a scalloped trim. As lovely gracing a simple slip dress as it is tossed over a black indie rock T-shirt, this shoulderette is a cozy piece of vintage charm.

Size

One size fits many

Finished Measurements

Width (top to bottom): 18" (45.5cm)

Length (cuff to cuff): 46" (116cm)

Materials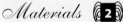

- Louet *Gems Sport Weight* (sport weight; 100% merino wool; 225 yd/206m per 3¾ oz/100g skein): 3 skeins Willow #55

- Size 5 (3.75mm) needles

- Size 7 (4.5mm) needles or size needed to obtain gauge

- Size F/5 (3.75mm) crochet hook

- Tapestry needle

Gauge

20 sts and 36 rows = 4" (10cm) in garter st on larger needles.

Adjust needle size as necessary to obtain correct gauge.

GARTER AND EYELETS (even number of sts)

Rows 1–30: Knit.

Row 31 (Eyelet row): K1, *k2tog, yo; rep from * to last st, k1.

Row 32: Knit.

Rep Rows 1–32 for pat.

Instructions

CUFF
With smaller needles, CO 50 sts, leaving a 20" (50.5cm) tail.

Row 1 (RS): K2, *p2, k2; rep from * across.

Work even in est rib until piece measures 3" (7.5cm), ending with a WS row.

BODY
Change to larger needles and work 4 rows in Garter and Eyelets pat.

Inc row (RS): K1 (selvedge st), k1b&f, knit to last 2 sts, k1b&f, k1 (selvedge st)—52 sts.

Cont in pat and rep Inc row [every 4 rows] 19 times, marking last Inc row—90 sts.

Work even until piece measures approx 34" (86.5cm) (or desired length), ending at the same point in the Garter and Eyelet pat as the last Inc row to ensure that second sleeve is a mirror image of first.

Dec row (RS): K1, ssk, knit to last 3 sts, k2tog, k1—88 sts.

Cont in Garter and Eyelet pat and rep Dec row [every 4 rows] 19 times—50 sts.

Work 3 rows even.

CUFF
Next row (RS): Change to smaller needles; k2, *p2, k2; rep from * across.

Work even in est rib for 3" (7.5cm), ending with a WS row.

BO loosely in rib.

Cut yarn leaving about 20" (50.5cm) tail to sew cuff and sleeve.

Finishing

Block to finished measurements.

With RS facing and using tail, sew cuff seam using mattress st, then sew underarm seam for 9" (22.5cm), invisibly weaving the garter st edges. Cut yarn leaving a 4" (10cm) tail.

Seam other cuff and sleeve.

- The project is worked cuff-to-cuff; the cuffs fall mid-arm.

- If an Inc or Dec row falls on an Eyelet Row, work the inc or dec in the row before the Eyelet row.

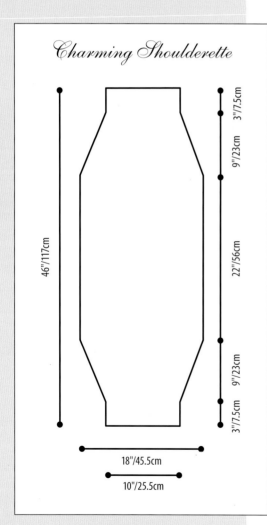

Charming Shoulderette

46"/117cm

3"/7.5cm

9"/23cm

22"/56cm

9"/23cm

3"/7.5cm

18"/45.5cm

10"/25.5cm

Edging

Join yarn at one end of opening.

With crochet hook, *sc in first garter ridge, skip next garter ridge and work [2 dc, ch 1, 2 dc] in the "valley" between next 2 ridges; rep from * around, alternating sc in ridges and dc clusters in valleys between ridges, adjusting spacing as necessary to allow crochet trim to lie flat.

Cut yarn leaving a 4" (10cm) tail and fasten off.

Work crochet trim around edge of each cuff, working scs between 2 knit sts and the dc clusters between 2 purl sts.

Cut yarn leaving a 4" (10cm) tail and fasten off.

Weave in all ends.

Sunday Gloves

Design by Sharon Hilchie

These lovely gloves capture the spirit of the days when stylishly dressed women wouldn't dream of leaving the house in their Sunday best without a pair. If you're new to lace, don't be intimidated; the two lace patterns used are very simple and the gloves are small, so they still work up quickly in the small gauge.

Sizes

Woman's extra-small (small, medium, large, extra-large)

Instructions are given for smallest size, with larger sizes in parentheses. When only 1 number is given, it applies to all sizes.

Finished Measurements

Hand circumference: 6½ (7, 7½, 8, 8½)"/16.5 (18, 19, 20.5, 21.5)cm

Length: 7 (7½, 8, 9, 9½)"/18 (19, 20.5, 23, 24)cm

Materials

- Knit Picks *Shadow* (lace weight; 100% merino wool; 440 yd/402m per 1¾ oz/50g hank): 1 hank each Vineyard Heather #23657 (MC) and Sunset Heather #23661 (CC)

- Size 2 (2.75mm) double-pointed needles (set of 5) or size needed to obtain gauge

- Waste yarn

- 2 stitch markers

Gauge

36 sts and 48 rnds = 4" (10cm) in St st.

Adjust needle size as necessary to obtain correct gauge.

Special Abbreviation

S2KP2 (center double decrease): Slip 2 sts as if to k2tog, k1, pass the 2 slipped sts over.

Special Technique

Jogless join: The jogless join technique is recommended when switching colors. To do this, work 1 rnd in new color and on the first st of the next rnd, pick up 1 st in the old color from 1 rnd below the color change and knit it together with the first st in the new color.

Pattern Notes

- The first several rows are worked back and forth to make a side vent. When worn, this vent will be at the outer wrist opposite the thumb.

- Leave long tails when casting on for fingers.

- Two 1¾oz (50g) skeins of yarn (MC and CC) should yield 4–5 pairs of gloves if you switch the colors.

Stitch Pattern

MAIN LACE PATTERN (multiple of 3 sts)
Rnd 1: *K1, yo, k2tog; rep from * around.

Rnd 2: Knit.

Rnd 3: *K1, ssk, yo; rep from * around.

Rnd 4: Knit.

Rep Rnds 1–4 for pat.

Instructions

RIGHT GLOVE
Lace trim
With CC, CO 37 (43, 49, 55, 61) sts; do not join.

Rows 1, 3, 5 (WS): Purl.

Rows 2, 4, 6 (RS): K1, *yo, k1, S2KP2, k1, yo, k1; rep from * around.

Wrist
Row 1 (WS): Switch to MC and purl across.

Row 2 (RS): Sl 1, knit to last st, dividing sts among 4 dpns.

Being careful not to twist sts, join to work in the round, slipping last st onto first dpn, then knitting the first st of rnd tog with the last st; mark beg of rnd—36 (42, 48, 54, 60) sts.

Knit 12 rnds.

Switch to CC.

Rnds 1 and 3: Knit.

Rnds 2 and 4: *K1, yo, k1, S2KP2, k1, yo; rep from * around.

Switch to MC, work 3 rnds in St st.

Hand
Beg Main Lace pat and work even until piece measures 1 (1, 1½, 1½, 2)"/2.5 (2.5, 4, 4, 5)cm from the color change, ending with an even rnd.

Thumb gusset
Set-up rnd: Work 18 (21, 24, 27, 30) sts in est pat, pm, work 6 sts in pat, pm, work 12 (15, 18, 21, 24) sts in pat.

Gusset Inc rnd: Knit to marker, slip marker, yo, knit to marker, yo, slip marker, knit to end—38 (44, 50, 56, 60) sts, with 8 sts between markers.

Work 3 rnds in est pat.

Rep [last 4 rnds] twice, working new gusset sts in St st until they can be integrated into the pat—42 (48, 54, 60, 66) sts.

Split for thumb

Next rnd: Knit to marker, remove marker, place 12 sts on waste yarn, CO 6 sts, remove marker, knit to end—36 (42, 48, 54, 60) sts.

Work even in est pat for 1 (1, 1, 1½, 1½)"/2.5 (2.5, 2.5, 4, 4)cm, ending with Rnd 4.

Split for little finger

Next rnd: K31 (35, 39, 45, 50), place next 10 (11, 14, 15, 16) sts on waste yarn for little finger (removing beg of rnd marker), CO 1 (2, 2, 3, 4) sts, pm for new beg of rnd—27 (33, 36, 42, 48) sts on needles.

Work 3 rnds in pat.

Ring finger

K3 (4, 5, 6, 7), place next 17 (21, 23, 27, 31) sts on waste yarn, CO 2 (3, 2, 3, 4), k7 (8, 8, 9, 10)—12 (15, 15, 18, 21) sts.

Work in pat for 2¼ (2½, 2¾, 3, 3¼)"/5.5 (6.5, 7, 7.5, 8.5)cm or to fit, ending with a knit rnd.

Next rnd: Work S2KP2 around; break yarn and thread through rem 4 (5, 5, 6, 7) sts, pulling tight.

Middle finger

Place 4 (5, 5, 6, 7) sts from first end of waste yarn onto needles, CO 3 (3, 3, 3, 4) sts, place 3 (4, 5, 6, 7) sts from other end of waste yarn onto needles, pick up and knit 2 (3, 2, 3, 3) sts from CO edge of ring finger—12 (15, 15, 18, 21) sts.

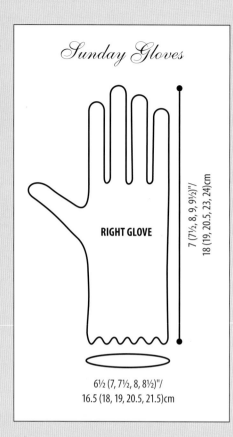

Sunday Gloves

RIGHT GLOVE

7 (7½, 8, 9, 9½)"/
18 (19, 20.5, 23, 24)cm

6½ (7, 7½, 8, 8½)"/
16.5 (18, 19, 20.5, 21.5)cm

Work in pat for 2½ (2¾, 3, 3¼, 3½)"/6.5 (7, 7.5, 8.5, 9)cm or to fit, ending with a knit rnd.

Next rnd: Work S2KP2 around; break yarn and thread through rem 4 (5, 5, 6, 7) sts, pulling tight.

Index finger
Place rem 10 (12, 13, 15, 17) sts from waste yarn onto needles, pick up and knit 2 (3, 2, 3, 4) sts from CO edge of middle finger—12 (15, 15, 18, 21) sts on needles.

Work in pat for 2 (2¼, 2½, 2¾, 3)"/5 (5.5, 6.5, 7, 7.5)cm or to fit, ending with a knit rnd.

Next rnd: Work S2KP2 around; break yarn and thread through rem 4 (5, 5, 6, 7) sts, pulling tight.

Little finger
Distribute 10 (11, 14, 15, 16) sts from waste yarn among dpns; pick up and knit 2 (1, 1, 3, 5) sts from CO edge of ring finger—12 (12, 15, 18, 21) sts on needles.

Work in pat for 1¾ (2, 2¼, 2½, 2¾)"/4.5 (5, 5.5, 6.5, 7)cm or to fit, ending with a knit rnd.

Next rnd: Work S2KP2 around; break yarn and pull tight through rem 4 (4, 5, 6, 7) sts.

Thumb
Distribute thumb gusset sts among the dpns; pick up and knit 7 (7, 10, 10, 10) sts across CO edge—19 (19, 22, 22, 22) sts.

Rnd 1: K11 (from sts that were on the waste yarn), S2KP2, k3 (3, 6, 6, 6) sts, S2KP2 (with first st from this round); mark new beg of rnd—15 (15, 18, 18, 18) sts on needles.

Work in pat for 1¾ (2, 2¼, 2½, 2¾)"/4.5 (5, 5.5, 6.5, 7)cm or to fit, ending with a knit rnd.

Next rnd: Work S2KP2 around; break yarn and pull tight through rem 5 (5, 6, 6, 6) sts.

LEFT GLOVE
Work as for right glove to thumb gusset.

Thumb gusset
Set-up rnd: Work 12 (15, 18, 21, 24) sts in est pat, pm, work 6 sts in pat, pm, work rem sts in pat.

Complete as for right glove.

Finishing

Weave in all ends, taking extra care to work tails in far enough to be secure.

Block to stretch out lace vertically.

Abbreviations

beg begin, beginning, begins

BO bind off

CC contrast color

ch chain

cm centimeter(s)

CO cast on

cont continue, continuing

dc double crochet

dec(s) decrease, decreasing, decreases

dpn double-pointed needle(s)

est establish, established

inc(s) increase(s), increasing

k knit

k1f&b knit into front then back of same st (increase)

k1-tbl knit 1 st through back loop

k2tog knit 2 sts together (decrease)

kwise knitwise (as if to knit)

LH left-hand

m(s) marker(s)

MC main color

mm millimeter(s)

M1 make 1 (increase)

M1k make 1 knitwise.

M1p make 1 purlwise

pat(s) pattern(s)

p purl

p1f&b purl into front then back of same st (increase)

p1-tbl purl 1 st through back loop

p2tog purl 2 sts together (decrease)

pm(s) place marker(s)

psso pass slip st(s) over

pwise purlwise (as if to purl)

rem remain(s), remaining

rep(s) repeat(s), repeated, repeating

RH right-hand

rib ribbing

rnd(s) round(s)

RS right side (of work)

rev sc reverse single crochet (crab st)

sc single crochet

sl slip, slipped, slipping

ssk [slip 1 st knitwise] twice from left needle to right needle, insert left needle tip into fronts of both slipped sts, knit both sts together from this position (left-leaning decrease)

ssp [slip 1 st knitwise] twice from left needle to right needle, return both sts to left needle and purl both together through back loops (left-leaning decrease)

st(s) stitch(es)

St st stockinette stitch

tbl through back loop

tog together

w&t wrap next stitch then turn work (often used in short rows)

WS wrong side (of work)

wyib with yarn in back

wyif with yarn in front

yb yarn back

yf yarn forward

yo yarn over

* repeat instructions from *

( ) alternate measurements and/or instructions

[ ] instructions to be worked as a group a specified number of times

Yarn Sources

Berroco, Inc.
www.berroco.com

Caron
www.caron.com

Cascade Yarns
www.cascadeyarns.com

Classic Elite
www.classiceliteyarns.com

Debbie Bliss
Distributed by Knitting Fever Inc.
www.knittingfever.com

Halcyon Yarn
http://halcyonyarn.com

Hand Maiden Fine Yarn
http://handmaiden.ca

J&P Coats
www.coatsandclark.com

Jamieson's
www.jamiesonsshetland.co.uk

Jo Sharp
www.josharp.com

KnitPicks
www.knitspicks.com

Lana Gatto
Distributed by Diamond Yarn
www.diamondyarn.com

Lily Chin
www.lilychinyarns.com

Loop-d-Loop
Distributed by Tahki Stacy Charles Inc.
www.tahkistacycharles.com

Lorna's Laces
www.lornaslaces.net

Louet North America
www.louet.com

Rowan
Distributed by Westminster Fibers
www.knitrowan.com

ShibuiKnits, LLC
www.shibuiknits.com

Stitch Diva Studios
www.stitchdiva.com

Stonehedge Fiber Mill
www.stonehedgefibermill.com

Tilli Tomas
www.tillitomas.com

Standard Yarn Weight System

Categories of yarn, gauge ranges, and recommended needle and hook sizes

Yarn Weight Symbol & Category Names	0 Lace	1 Super Fine	2 Fine	3 Light	4 Medium	5 Bulky	6 Super Bulky
Type of Yarns in Category	Fingering 10 count crochet thread	Sock, Fingering, Baby	Sport, Baby	DK, Light Worsted	Worsted, Afghan, Aran	Chunky, Craft, Rug	Bulky, Roving
Knit Gauge Range* in Stockinette Stitch to 4 inches	33–40** sts	27–32 sts	23–26 sts	21–24 sts	16–20 sts	12–15 sts	6–11 sts
Recommended Needle in Metric Size Range	1.5–2.25 mm	2.25–3.25 mm	3.25–3.75 mm	3.75–4.5 mm	4.5–5.5 mm	5.5–8 mm	8 mm and larger
Recommended Needle U.S. Size Range	000 to 1	1 to 3	3 to 5	5 to 7	7 to 9	9 to 11	11 and larger
Crochet Gauge* Ranges in Single Crochet to 4 inch	32-42 double crochets**	21–32 sts	16–20 sts	12–17 sts	11–14 sts	8–11 sts	5–9 sts
Recommended Hook in Metric Size Range	Steel*** 1.6–1.4mm Regular hook 2.25 mm	2.25–3.5 mm	3.5–4.5 mm	4.5–5.5 mm	5.5–6.5 mm	6.5–9 mm	9 mm and larger
Recommended Hook U.S. Size Range	Steel*** 6, 7, 8 Regular hook B–1	B–1 to E–4	E–4 to 7	7 to I–9	I–9 to K–10½	K–10½ to M–13	M–13 and larger

* GUIDELINES ONLY: The above reflect the most commonly used gauges and needle or hook sizes for specific yarn categories.

** Lace weight yarns are usually knitted or crocheted on larger needles and hooks to create lacy, openwork patterns. Accordingly, a gauge range is difficult to determine. Always follow the gauge stated in your pattern.

*** Steel crochet hooks are sized differently from regular hooks--the higher the number, the smaller the hook, which is the reverse of regular hook sizing.

This Standards & Guidelines booklet and downloadable symbol artwork are available at: **YarnStandards.com**

About the Designers

Anna Bell has been knitting since childhood and designing knitwear since 2005. She lives and works in London and is the current editor of *Yarn Forward* magazine. See more of her work at http://needleandhook.co.uk.

An award-winning educator at the college/university level with an MFA in creative writing and a Ph.D. in English Renaissance Literature, **Nora J. Bellows** began creating one-of-a-kind, felted bags with original felted flowers under the brand name Noni® in 2001, shortly after discovering knitted felt. Nora's felted designs have appeared in several publications in the United States and Britain, including *Interweave Felt, Knitting Today* (UK), and *Simply Knitting* (UK). She teaches intensive, hands-on knitting and felting workshops across the country.

Ellen Brys studied fashion design in New York and London and has specialized in sweater design for most of her career. She taught herself to crochet at age twelve and has sold designs to major fashion companies in the United States and Europe. Her collection of vintage needlework and textiles provides inspiration for many of her designs.

Former wilderness ranger, environmental activist, and organic farmer for the past twenty-four years, **MaryJane Butters** has worn many hats (and aprons) in her day, but none more proudly than that of modern-day farmgirl. She is the author of three books, including *MaryJane's Ideabook, Cookbook, Lifebook for the Farmgirl in All of Us* (Clarkson Potter, 2005), and *MaryJane's Stitching Room* (Clarkson Potter, 2007). She publishes her own magazine, *MaryJane's Farm,* and designs organic bed linens and fabrics that are available worldwide.

Tatyana T. Chambers was born and raised in Russia, where she lived in the ancient city of Astrakhan on the Volga River. Tatyana learned to knit from a neighbor when she was six years old, and she has been knitting on and off ever since. Later she taught herself to crochet and felt, and she began designing her own accessories using a variety of knitting and felting techniques. Tatyana studied art and worked as a graphic designer until 2004, when she met her future husband, David, and moved to the United States. Tatyana now lives in Alexandria, Virginia, where she runs her own business, Wool Thumb Creations, designing hand-crafted accessories made from wool for women and home. You can find Tatyana's designs on Etsy.com.

Lily M. Chin is an internationally famous knitter and crocheter who has worked in the yarn industry for more than twenty-five years as a designer, instructor, and author of books on knitting and crochet. She has created couture crochet for the New York Fashion Week runway collections of designers Ralph Lauren, Vera Wang, Diane von Furstenberg, and Isaac Mizrahi, and her work has been on the backs of celebrities and supermodels from Racquel Welch and Vanna White to Cindy Crawford and Naomi Campbell. Visit her website at www.lilychinsignaturecollection.com.

Betty Christiansen is the author of *Knitting for Peace: Make the World a Better Place One Stitch at a Time* (STC Craft, 2006) and has written for *Interweave Knits, Vogue Knitting,* and *Family Circle Easy Knitting.* She lives in La Crosse, Wisconsin, with her husband, Andrew, and her small children, Eliot and Ivy, and where she is the editor of *Coulee Region Women,* the area's women's magazine. She fondly remembers the days when she had time to knit.

Teva Durham grew up in St. Louis, Missouri, with rather unconventional parents who had met in art school. As a teenager, she moved to New York City, attended the High School of Performing Arts, and collected vintage clothing for costumes. Teva developed a particular fondness for sweaters culled from Lower Manhattan thrift shops and soon took up knitting. After pursuing acting and then journalism, Teva made a career out of her obsessive hobby and launched one of the first online knitting pattern sites, loop-d-loop.com, in 2000. She is the author of *Loop-d-Loop* (STC Craft, 2005) and *Loop-d-Loop Crochet* (STC Craft, 2007) and produces a line of yarns distributed by Tahki Stacy Charles.

Gretchen Funk lives and knits in Minnesota, where she and her husband own and operate the Triple Rock Social Club. She teaches knitting at The Yarnery in St. Paul, MN and at Crafty Planet, a needlework and craft shop in Minneapolis.

Franklin Habit is a designer, writer, and illustrator who lives in Chicago. He is the author of *It Itches: A Stash of Knitting Cartoons,* and his work has appeared in *Interweave Knits, Interweave Crochet, Yarn Market News, Vogue Knitting,* Knitty.com, and TwistCollective.com. He chronicles his adventures in his blog at the-panopticon.blogspot.com.

Jennifer Hansen is the founder and chief designer of Stitch Diva Studios. She lives in Fremont, California, where she is a full-time crochet and knit designer, teacher, and writer. Her innovative crochet work has been featured in various books, magazines, and television shows, including *Vogue Knitting, Interweave Crochet, The Happy Hooker, The Encyclopedia of Crochet,* and *Knitty Gritty.*

A licensed pilot and electrical engineer, **Sharon Hilchie** learned to knit from the same woman who taught her to fly sailplanes. She will be showing off her knitting stuff at www.knitiverse.com.

Andrea M. Holliger is a scholar of nineteenth-century American literature, currently pursuing a Ph.D. and teaching at the University of Kentucky. She has been knitting for most of her life, but only recently discovered her passion for vintage styles. In addition to designing vintage-inspired patterns, she also offers vintage reproductions and recycled yarns, and maintains a vintage blog at www.SweaterGirlKnit.com.

Susan Pierce Lawrence learned to knit as a child and rediscovered the craft during her last year of law school. She is infatuated with knitting lace and finds inspiration in the mountainous region surrounding her home near the Wasatch Mountains in Utah.

Three years ago, **Elanor Lynn** relocated from Brooklyn, New York, to Hollywood, California. Since then, she's been knitting lots of palm trees into tapestries. She's currently exploring "handwritten" fonts in text-based work.

A native of Ohio, **Annie Modesitt** taught herself to knit at age twenty-five, before a move from New York City to Texas. The Texas tenure didn't last, but knitting did, and upon her return to the New York area, Annie began knitting for other designers and designing for major knitting magazines. Her work has appeared in *Interweave Knits, Vogue Knitting, Knitters Magazine, Cast On, Family Circle Easy Knitting, McCalls Needlework,* and several family-oriented magazines.

Michele Rose Orne began knitting at age five, when she was taught by her mother and Dutch grandmother. She graduated from Yale in 1985 and worked as a designer in New York for five years before moving to Maine. Her knitwear designs have appeared in *Vogue Knitting* and *Interweave Knits,* and she has created many patterns for yarn companies, such as Classic Elite, Tahki, Reynolds, and Nashua. She recently published her first book of patterns, *Inspired to Knit* (Interweave Press, 2008).

Kristin Spurkland learned to knit from her roommate, Sophie, in her freshman year of college. In 1998, she received her degree in apparel design from Bassist College in Portland, Oregon, and decided to pursue a career in knitwear design. She has been designing ever since. Kristin is the author of four books, including *The Knitting Man(ual)* (Ten Speed Press, 2007).

Melissa Wehrle learned to knit from her grandmother when she was seven years old, but she quickly lost interest in making Barbie tube dresses and put down the needles for several years. Her passion was renewed when she moved to New York City to study at the Fashion Institute of Technology, where she majored in fashion design and specialized in knitwear. Melissa graduated from FIT in May 2002 and has worked as a knitwear designer in the industry ever since. She is the junior/ contemporary designer for a sweater manufacturer in New York City. In her free time, she designs for magazines, for small yarn companies, and for her own line of hand-knit patterns called neoknits. She is also the creative director for One Planet Yarn and Fiber. Melissa's current projects and designs in progress can be viewed at her website: neoknits.com.

Index